MW01196017

A FalconGuide® to
Mammoth Cave National Park

Help Us Keep This Guide Up to Date

Every effort has been made by the author and editors to make this guide as accurate and useful as possible. However, many things can change after a guide is published—trails are rerouted, regulations change, techniques evolve, facilities come under new management, and so on.

We would love to hear from you concerning your experiences with this guide and how you feel it could be improved and kept up to date. While we may not be able to respond to all comments and suggestions, we'll take them to heart and we'll also make certain to share them with the author. Please send your comments and suggestions to the following address:

The Globe Pequot Press
Reader Response/Editorial Department
P.O. Box 480
Guilford, CT 06437

Or you may e-mail us at:

editorial@GlobePequot.com

Thanks for your input, and happy trails!

A **FALCON** GUIDE®

Exploring Series

A FalconGuide® to Mammoth Cave National Park

A Guide to Exploring the Caves, Trails, Roads, and Rivers

Johnny Molloy

FALCON GUIDE®

GUILFORD, CONNECTICUT
HELENA, MONTANA

AN IMPRINT OF THE GLOBE PEQUOT PRESS

Copyright © 2006 Morris Book Publishing, LLC

All rights reserved. No part of this book may be reproduced or transmitted in any form by any means, electronic or mechanical, including photocopying and recording, or by any information storage and retrieval system, except as may be expressly permitted by the 1976 Copyright Act or by the publisher. Requests for permission should be made in writing to The Globe Pequot Press, P.O. Box 480, Guilford, Connecticut 06437.

Falcon and FalconGuide are registered trademarks of Morris Book Publishing, LLC.

Maps created by Trailhead Graphics © Morris Book Publishing, LLC
Photo credits: Photos on pages 14, 19, 24, 30 courtesy of the National Park Service. All other photos by Johnny Molloy.

Library of Congress Cataloging-in-Publication Data
Molloy, Johnny, 1961–
    A FalconGuide to Mammoth Cave National Park: a guide to exploring the caves, trails, roads, and rivers / Johnny Molloy. — 1st ed.
        p. cm. — (Exploring series)
    Cover title: Mammoth Cave National Park
    Includes index.
    ISBN-13: 978-0-7627-3997-4
    ISBN-10: 0-7627-3997-5
    1. Caving—Kentucky—Mammoth Cave. 2. Mammoth Cave (Ky.)—Discovery and exploration. 3. Mammoth Cave National Park (Ky.)—Guidebooks. I. Title. II. Title: Falcon Guide to Mammoth Cave National Park. III. Title: Mammoth Cave National Park. IV. Series.
    GV200.655.K42M256 2006
    796.52'509769754—dc22

                                                                2006012776

Manufactured in the United States of America
First Edition/First Printing

To buy books in quantity for corporate use
or incentives, call **(800) 962–0973, ext. 4551,**
or e-mail **premiums@GlobePequot.com.**

The author and The Globe Pequot Press assume no liability for accidents happening to, or injuries sustained by, readers who engage in the activities described in this book.

This book is for all the people who have explored the passages of Mammoth Cave and for all the people who will explore the unseen passages to come.

Contents

Acknowledgments

The staff at Mammoth Cave National Park was the best ever to work with. These Kentuckians made writing this book more fun and easier than it otherwise would have been. From the people in the visitor center to the behind-the-scenes folk, everyone helped however they could. Specifically I would like to thank Mike Adams for his enthusiasm, and Leslie Lewis and Cindy Logsdon for their wonderful help and friendship. All the guides on the cave tours made learning about Mammoth Cave that much better, especially Colleen Olsen and Ronnie Doyle. Also, thanks to Beverly Scoggins and Kathy Proffitt for helping. Thanks to Linda Guess at the bookstore for her all-around friendliness. Thanks also to Jim Norris, Adam Turner, Brandy Button, and Joyce Hester for their help.

Thanks to my brothers Mike and Steele for coming up and exploring the park with me; Matt, too, for catching that big bass on the Green River. Thanks to Tina Dean, along with her brother Greg and sister-in-law Anja, for traveling the Green, too. Thanks to my friends John Cox and Steve "Devo" Grayson for going backpacking with me in the backcountry. Thanks to the women of Bowling Green, Alisa, Ashley, Jayne, Lisa, and Natalie, for their love of Kentucky.

Introducing Mammoth Cave National Park

Mammoth Cave National Park is a world-renowned American treasure. Simply put, this is the largest, longest known cave in the world, with more than twenty-four openings and 365 miles of mapped passageways, and many more miles yet to be discovered. It is a place where darkness rules and time moves at the pace of the water slowly dissolving its limestone walls, creating more passageways to be discovered by future generations. It is a place of large rooms, high domes, tight passages, long avenues, and strange formations; a place where occasional waterfalls, lakes, and rivers flow beneath a verdant cover of south-central Kentucky woodland.

A Brief History of Mammoth Cave

Today's tour groups and the ranger-guides who lead them are following thousands upon thousands of footfalls that echoed off the walls before them. Mammoth Cave was first discovered by aboriginals more than 4,000 years ago. We know this from carbon-dating the torches they left, burned to hand level and discarded in the cave. These torches were reeds of cane, gathered from the nearby Green River and tied together. It took many such lights to work far back into the cave, where Natives chiseled sparkling gypsum off the cave walls, using

The Cave City Entrance to Mammoth Cave National Park welcomes visitors and is the backdrop for many photos.

it for reasons unknown to us. And for 2,000 years they explored Mammoth Cave, leaving other archaeological evidence of their presence. Then they stopped entering the cave. We don't know why.

And for nearly two millennia Mammoth Cave was left to the cave spiders, eyeless fish, and crayfish that live underneath the land, along with sporadic forays by four-legged visitors that could only temporarily take the constant fifty-four-degree temperature, the silence, and most of all the darkness, a darkness so black it cannot be experienced on the land surface. Then, legend has it, a Kentucky resident named John Houchins was hunting bear in the region, back in the 1790s. He wounded a bear and chased it into what is now known as the Historic Entrance into Mammoth Cave. Houchins promptly forgot all about the bear and went a-cavin', at least according to the legend. Mammoth Cave was found again.

And we enter the modern era of Mammoth Cave. Interestingly, it was the economic potential of the underworld that initially brought the cave fame. The dirt below was rich in saltpeter, a necessary component in the making of gunpowder. Our young nation was blockaded by England, thus halting imports of saltpeter, and we needed munitions. The War of 1812 was imminent and slaves were put to work in the cave, extracting saltpeter using primitive wood operations: vats and wooden pipes that still exist to this day in the preservative atmosphere of the cave. This national resource became known across America; people began visiting Mammoth Cave, and tour operations were set up, making this parcel of underground Kentucky one of the oldest tourist destinations in American history.

Back then guides led tours using lanterns lit with animal fat and anything else that would burn. Along with markings from the aboriginals, the tops of passageways were blackened by smoke, and visitors were urged to write upon the cave. At this time many cave guides became famous themselves. The most renowned of them all was Stephen Bishop, a slave who made daring explorations of previously unknown passages, in addition to putting on cave tours with flair.

The land above Mammoth Cave became valuable, because those who controlled it enjoyed the fruits from down below. Men sought fortunes from tourism, and maybe saltpeter again. Aboveground, accommodations sprung up to serve tourists in search of food and lodging. The land over the cave changed hands. In addition, railroad service was completed to Mammoth Cave and steamboats plied the Green River, taking tourists from Evansville, Indiana, to visit the cave.

As time passed, tourist dollars became more and more important, ushering in the "Kentucky Cave Wars." As the known part of Mammoth Cave began to increase in size, and with the discovery of other area caves, local residents and landowners began hawking their caves as the best to visit and as part of Mammoth Cave, sometimes confusing tourists (an easy thing to do, no matter where

Dr. Croghan's Grand Experiment

In 1839 one Dr. John Croghan bought a large tract of land that included Mammoth Cave. He then set up a tuberculosis hospital deep in the cave, believing its atmosphere would help patients. As it turned out, however, the chill and the fires—which burned around the clock to keep the patients warm—may have actually hastened their demise. The ruins of Croghan's experiment can still be seen. The doctor himself lived until 1849, then left a complicated will that wasn't completely settled until his last heir died in 1926.

they visit). Landowners began to realize some cave tours that began on adjacent property led under their property, and sued for profits. New entrances were blasted into the cave, and the courts were clogged with lawsuits.

Then came Floyd Collins, cave explorer extraordinaire. In trying to develop a tourist cave along the route to Mammoth—the cave his family was hawking was off the beaten path—Floyd entered Sand Cave and became trapped by fallen rock. And there he lay. While those aboveground tried to rescue him, a nation became entranced with his story, bringing such crowds that the National Guard was called out to handle them. Unfortunately, Collins died before he could be rescued, but Mammoth Cave was once again on the national stage.

At the same time, a movement to establish national parks east of the Mississippi River in the grand tradition of Yellowstone to the west began gathering momentum. Some suggested there should be a Mammoth Cave National Park. Problem was, the land above the potential park was privately owned, not already owned by the federal government, as was Yellowstone. The state of Kentucky began raising money to buy the land above and around the Mammoth Cave. The national park model at the time was that of a grandiose wilderness. Some land was acquired around the cave, but the Department of the Interior insisted that the project fit the national park model, which meant that more land had to be pieced together. In the end more than 50,000 acres were set aside. Still, aboveground this land was far from wilderness: It was mostly cleared, tilled by farmers who had been there for generations. Understandably, many of these settlers didn't want to leave, but ultimately they were all forced off their lands. The same thing was going on in the Great Smoky Mountains and Shenandoah, two other eastern destinations that became parks. In came the Civilian Conservation Corps, tearing down houses, planting trees, and developing the park above- and belowground, where they made cave trails, created walkways, and strung lights.

Although completion had to wait for World War II to end, Mammoth Cave National Park was finally dedicated in 1946. And since its inception the park has continued to evolve, modernizing its facilities above- and belowground. Descendants of former area residents now work here. And another generation of park visitors takes their offspring to see the cave, continuing a tradition—and building a foundation of people who see Mammoth Cave as not just a park but an American icon, and a place we can all hold dear.

An Overview of Recreation at the Park

Mammoth Cave National Park offers myriad recreation opportunities above- and belowground. This alone makes the park a rarity. But there's more to this spot's uniqueness. Most other parks preserve superlative terra firma, where the tallest mountains reach for the sky, arches bend over colorful rock, or scenic shorelines curve into the distance. The land above Mammoth Cave, however—while integral to the underworld below—is unusual in its own right. There are, for one thing, no other contiguous protected parcels of middle American upland hardwood forest of this size. Add the fact that this is "karst country," a land cut by a complex of fissures, caves, sinks, and bluffs centered by the Green River, which flows through the heart of the park.

So what does this means for the Mammoth Cave visitor? It means a national park ready to be experienced in any number of ways. The cave itself offers a sort of "inside-out" view of the area, while the Green River forms a water trail, a moving venue with a bottom-up view. You can enjoy this in your own boat or take a scenic guided boat tour. The hiking and equestrian trails of Mammoth Cave, meantime, offer top-down views, such as the one along the Green River Bluffs Trail. Or you can combine park history with pedaling on the Mammoth Cave Railroad Bike and Hike Trail, which traces a portion of the old railroad grade that once led passengers to the park. Maybe road biking along the quiet park roads is your bag, or maybe taking a scenic drive, horseback riding, or fishing on the Green River. Perhaps you want to combine your visit with camping outdoors—or maybe you prefer to enjoy the luxurious accommodations within the park boundaries. All these options, and more, are detailed in this book.

But most park visits begins with Mammoth Cave itself. Varieties of cave tours offer different perspectives on the underworld. You can learn about the past on the Historic Tour, or get a real taste of days gone by on the Violet City Lantern Tour, illuminated only by the primitive lights you'll carry yourself. The Grand Avenue Tour travels 4 miles, making for an underground "hike." And there is the Wild Cave Tour, where you get down and dirty, crawl through narrow passageways, and remain hunched over for surprising distances in addition to long walks along longer avenues. Cave tours last anywhere from just over an hour on up to six hours. Group sizes vary as well, from large-group short-in-length tours, such as the New Entrance Tour, to the small groups taken on the Introduction to Caving Tour. Other tours, such as the Trog Tour, are for kids only. After reading through the tour descriptions in this book, I promise you'll find a tour to suit your desires.

Mammoth Cave National Park comprises an impressive 53,000 acres. It covers much of Mammoth Cave below and is centered on the Green River, which flows east to west through the park. The land south of the Green is more developed, and is the location of the visitor center/hotel/park headquarters complex. This is where cave tours begin, and where facilities lie. Interpretive trails wind throughout the area, allowing you to peer out from a high bluff, or into the Historic Entrance to Mammoth Cave; you can see wildflower-covered spring bottomland, or Mammoth Dome Sink, or the River Styx as it emerges

Mammoth Cave's Historic Entrance is a major portal into Kentucky's underground wonderland.

from Mammoth Cave. It is a place to learn about the interrelationships among land, water, and cave. Other interpretive trails are located outside the visitor center area, such as Cedar Sink, a singularly impressive spot that is one of the most beautiful in the park.

And then there is the north side of the Green River, where a network of more than 70 miles of trails winding among hills and hollows can be enjoyed by hikers, bikers, and equestrians. Here, where nature has reclaimed former farmland, you can glimpse wildflowers growing alongside a crumbled sandstone chimney. Overhanging rocks form rockhouses more commonly seen in eastern Kentucky; springs emerge from underneath hills; water disappears into sinks. Trails travel along waterways, atop ridges, and past pioneer cemeteries. Luckily for backpackers, twelve designated backcountry campsites are situated along these trails, allowing for overnight enjoyment of this area.

The Green River and its major area feeder stream, the Nolin River, allow for watery exploration of the park, primarily by canoe and kayak, but also by small johnboats. Water travelers can see caves, bluffs, springs, and rich woods rife with wildlife. Camping is an option here, too, on gravel bars and islands in the river. Three developed campgrounds complement the backcountry camping opportunities. You can enjoy the convenience of Headquarters Campground, or rough it at Houchins Ferry. Or you might choose to camp with like-minded folks at Maple Springs Group Camp.

It's my hope that this book will spare you the tiring and sometimes frustrating task of researching everything available at the Mammoth Cave National Park, leaving you time to enjoy all the beauty this swath of Kentucky has to offer.

Mammoth Cave National Park Weather

It's always fifty-four degrees inside the cave, but aboveground weather varies. The climate here is seasonal, with warm to hot summers and moderate winters. Early spring is the most variable, with periodic warm-ups broken by cold fronts bringing rain, then chilly temperatures. Later on, temperatures stay warm; things get downright hot by July. Typically, mornings start clear, then clouds build and hit-or-miss thunderstorms occur by afternoon. The first cool fronts hit Mammoth Cave around mid-September. Fall sees warm clear days and cool nights with the least amount of rain, though rain amounts are somewhat steady throughout the year. Precipitation picks up in November, and temperatures generally stay cool to cold, broken by occasional mild spells. Snowfall varies winter to winter but averages less than 15 inches per year.

Weather Averages

The following chart lists monthly average temperatures and precipitation amounts for Glasgow, Kentucky—very near the park.

Month	Average High	Average Low	Mean Temp	Average Precip
January	46	26	36	4.3 inches
February	52	30	41	4.3 inches
March	62	38	50	5.1 inches
April	72	45	59	4.4 inches
May	80	54	67	5.3 inches
June	87	63	75	4.9 inches
July	91	67	79	4.8 inches
August	89	65	77	4.0 inches
September	83	58	71	4.0 inches
October	72	46	59	3.2 inches
November	60	38	49	4.5 inches
December	50	30	40	5.1 inches

How to Use This Guidebook

This book comprehensively and systematically covers potential activities at Mammoth Cave National Park. For starters, every cave tour is detailed, as is every marked and maintained aboveground trail. Following the trails are various other potential activities at Mammoth Cave, including bicycling, scenic driving, paddling, fishing, and boating.

"Where to Lay Your Head" details backcountry campsites, campgrounds, park accommodations, and area bed-and-breakfasts. "More Services and Resources for Explorers" is a bit of a grab-bag chapter, listing everything else you might need to know to enjoy a perfect stay here—from the park's many picnic areas to nearby towns, eateries, and more. Need gear or a shuttle? This chapter's list of outfitters will tell you who has what and who can give you a ride.

Hopefully, this book will make you appreciate and enjoy Mammoth Cave so much, you'll want to volunteer to keep it a great place. In case this happens, I've noted the contact information you'll need.

The Maps

You'll find a FalconGuide® four-color fold-out map provided at the back of this book. The front side of our map offers an overview of the entire national park with an accompanying map legend and a hypsometric key. The reverse side includes a regional map that shows how to drive to the park as well as a close-up of the area surrounding the visitor center.

In the accompanying FalconGuide® maps all trail positioning has been verified using a hand-held Global Positioning System (GPS) device for the greatest possible accuracy. Our maps also contain considerable detail, such as topography that shows both land and water features with the land elevation measured in feet. In addition you'll find numerous activity icons on the maps highlighting the visitor center, cave entrances, hiking trailheads, overlooks, bike trails, boat launches and put-ins, plus where to find ferries, a boat tour, and a bus tour. Lodgings, campgrounds, backcountry campsites, and picnic areas are also depicted on the maps. For your convenience the park overview map includes river miles as well as the distance in miles between towns.

A few notes about reading the topography: All three of our maps use shaded, or shadow, relief. *Shadow relief* does not represent elevation: It demonstrates slope or relative steepness. This gives an almost 3-D perspective of the physical geography of a region and will help you see where the ranges and valleys are.

The two larger-scale maps—the park overview and the regional map—employ a technique called *hypsometry*, which uses elevation tints to portray relief. Each tone represents a range of equal elevation, as shown in the hypsometric key on the map. These maps will give you a good idea of elevation gain and loss. The color tones shown on the bottom of the key represent lower elevations while the tones toward the top represent higher elevations. Narrow bands of different tones spaced closely together indicate steep terrain, whereas wider bands indicate areas of more gradual slope.

If you'd like to supplement our maps with a more detailed map for backcountry travel, you may want to obtain National Geographic's larger-scale map or you may prefer the 7.5-minute series of topographic maps published by the U.S. Geological Survey (USGS). Electronic versions of these maps can be found online or as packaged software. USGS maps are derived from aerial photos and are extremely accurate when it comes to terrain and natural features, but because the *topos*, as they are known, are not revised very often, trail, road, and other man-made features are often out of date. Even so, the 7.5-minute topo's fine depiction of topography is useful for seeing greater detail.

Favorite Sights and Scenes at Mammoth Cave

Mammoth Cave is full of beauty. However, beauty is in the eye of the beholder, as the saying goes. While one person might desire a fascinating cave tour, another might want to see a variety of wildflowers. Yet another might want to travel beneath a towering forest. After exploring the entire recreation area, here are some of my favorite Mammoth Cave experiences:

- Feeling the cool air blow from the Historic Entrance in summer.
- Seeing the jonquils bloom at all the old homesites in March.
- Seeing the gypsum sparkle by lantern light in Great Onyx Cave.
- Coasting along the Mammoth Cave Railroad Bike and Hike Trail after a fall rain.
- Watching the blooming dogwoods light up the forest.
- Coming out of the Historic Entrance to the cave and being bathed in moonlight.
- Eating lunch in the Snowball Room.
- Hearing then seeing a waterfall in Raymer Hollow.
- Taking a hot shower after the Wild Cave Tour.
- Seeing fall leaves blow onto the Good Spring Church Cemetery.
- Hearing wild turkeys gobble at sunrise.
- Bantering with friendly park rangers.
- Eating breakfast at the park hotel.
- Getting to know fellow visitors on the cave tours.
- Catching an 18-inch smallmouth bass on the Green River.
- Getting to know the neighbors in Headquarters Campground.
- Climbing the stairs inside Mammoth Dome.
- Sitting through an intentional blackout deep inside the cave.
- Seeing deer bound across Houchins Ferry Road during a scenic drive.
- Learning something new during a summertime ranger-led inter-pretive program.
- Riding the bus from the visitor center to the Frozen Niagara cave entrance.
- Sweltering in the campground on a hot summer day.
- Enjoying fall colors from the *Miss Green River II*.
- Being amazed at the number and variety of spring wildflowers.

Exploring Belowground:
The Caves

Mammoth Cave, the reason this national park exists, is a complex intertwined system of passages—a limestone labyrinth, if you will—with an extent that is simply unknown. As of this writing twenty-four cave entrances and 365 miles of passageways have been discovered and mapped, with many more miles to come. Still, this is already the longest known cave on the planet, truly deserving of the name *Mammoth*.

We mere mortals must leave future discoveries to experienced and accomplished spelunkers, as cavers as also known. But we can make our own personal discoveries of Mammoth Cave via the many cave tours offered at the park. These tours range from belowground quarter-mile strolls doable by almost everyone to miles-long wild cave tours in which you and your fellow cavers crawl through narrow, wet openings far removed from the wide passageways of other tours. Time lengths of tours vary, as do specific tour offerings. Call ahead to make sure the tour you desire is being offered when you plan your visit. Some tours can be reserved—and reservations are strongly recommended between April and October.

A tour group gathers and listens to the ranger tour guide before heading into the Historic Entrance to Mammoth Cave National Park.

Read through the tour descriptions in this chapter and find one suited to your abilities and desires. Knowledgeable guides, who are also park rangers, are there to lead you every step of the way, not only showing you the actual route but also informing you of the cave's human and natural history. Tours do cost money, and fees vary by tour length and duration. Certain tours have age limits, so read carefully before embarking on the tour of your choice.

The same tour can vary year to year, season to season, and even day to day. The makeup of the group and each particular guide can make every tour different. For example, tours in summer may include more children—and children can of course be talkative, irritating some of those who want to listen. So many tours are held in summer that the ticket office and visitor center can seem like a zoo, with various groups meeting in different places; it can be confusing. During the off-seasons, however—particularly winter and spring—tour groups are generally smaller and made up largely of adults. Those who really want to listen to and learn from the tour guides are more apt to succeed. Some tour guides are great storytellers and can work the crowds like the tent revival preachers who came through south-central Kentucky before this area was a park. Others are more science-oriented and stick to the facts. Each tour guide may point out features he or she finds particularly interesting that a different guide won't mention. Hopefully you will find your group and tour guide to your liking.

Enjoying the Underground World

The following tips should help make your visit to Mammoth Cave the best it can be.

Match a Tour with Your Physical Capabilities

Your time is valuable and you are spending hard-earned money to see the wonders of Mammoth Cave, so don't pay for a tour that you can't complete or won't enjoy. Some tours go into tightly enclosed places; others require extensive stooping. Do not let others talk you into a tour that you're uncomfortable with or are physically incapable of completing.

Be Smart in Your Footwear and Attire

Belowground trails can be bumpy and uneven. I have seen folks twist an ankle during tours. There are also many wet stairs. Wear sturdy, comfortable shoes— the kind you might use for a hiking trip. The cave temperature is fifty-four degrees, cooler or warmer near openings, and more constant the deeper you go in the cave. Dress appropriately. Walking will warm you, but remember that every tour includes portions where you stand still. I suggest long pants, a long-sleeved shirt, and a very light jacket. Add more clothing if you are cold-natured, less if you are warm-natured.

Don't Be Shy

Mammoth Cave is an intriguing place to visit and is sure to bring up any number of questions—everything from *What is that . . . ?* to *How on earth . . . ?* to (yes) *Where's the restroom?* Don't hesitate to ask your tour guide or any park rangers you spot about anything that's puzzling you. Park staff welcome inquisitive visitors.

A park ranger forms a silhouette in front of the New Entrance Domes.

Don't Bring the No-Nos

There is a specific list of things you cannot bring into the cave, some due to Homeland Security guidelines. If you bring them anyway, you will not be allowed to join your chosen tour. Here's what you *cannot* bring into the cave:

- Camera cases or tripods
- Backpacks, fanny packs, or child-carrying backpacks
- Baby strollers
- Diaper bags
- Purses
- Guns
- Knives
- Mace

The Park Service does have lockers installed to store most of the above items. You will have to keep your camera in your pocket or around your neck. A strap is very handy here. Walking canes are allowed only if they are demonstrably needed. Leave the smokes behind, too, as no smoking is allowed in the cave. One more thing: Pets are forbidden in the cave, and the park frowns on leaving dogs in the parking lot (which is a bad idea anyway). Kennels are available to keep your pet. Contact the park lodge desk at (270) 758–2225 for more information.

Underground Camera Savvy

Few photographers have extensive experience taking underground pictures, so have realistic expectations. Using a flash will result in less blurry pictures, but be conscious of other cave visitors and don't blind them. Be aware that flash photography is discouraged on lantern tours, as the flash disrupts the eye's ability to adjust to the dark. Handrails can help still your hands for nonflash photos. Big rooms underground dissipate light; try to get 12 feet or closer to objects. Video cameras are allowed, but stop before you film, and leave the high-intensity lighting behind in consideration of other cave visitors. Do not try to film or take pictures while on the move. Cave visitors with video and still cameras are statistically more likely to have accidents because they often fail to look where they're going—or try to navigate their way through a lens. That's a fool's game.

Reservations

Cave tours are the most popular visitor activity at Mammoth Cave National Park. They can sell out quickly, especially at peak visitation in summer. Reservations are highly recommended during this time, or if you have limited time during your park visit. There are three ways to make reservations: by phone, by fax, and on the Internet. The phone reservation number is (800) 967–2283. The international phone number is (301) 722–1257. The reservation call center is open from 9:00 A.M. to 9:00 P.M. Central Time, seven days a week. For reservations on the Internet, visit www.reservations.nps.gov.

Cave Tours

New Entrance Tour

DURATION OF TOUR: 2 hours

DISTANCE COVERED: 0.75 mile

TOUR SIZE LIMIT: 118

DIFFICULTY: Moderate

AGE LIMIT: None

HIGHLIGHTS: Roosevelt's Dome, Grand Central Station, Fairy Ceiling, Crystal Lake, Frozen Niagara, Drapery Room, waterfall

This tour starts in one entrance and comes out another, eliminating the need to backtrack. A 4-mile bus ride leads to the New Entrance, which was widened and enhanced with stairs in 1921 to allow people to enter more easily. Cave explorers get an immediate surprise as they descend into a dripping deep pit, where stainless-steel metal stairs lead between slender passages and past interesting rock formations. The water dripping around you (and onto you, a little bit) is what formed the features through which you're walking, and adds an adventurous aura to the affair. You'll negotiate a total of 300 stairs before leveling out 250 feet below the surface at Grand Central Station—so named for the six ways into and out of the large room, just as in New York City's famed landmark. Here the ranger-guide continues to inform neophyte cave people about their new surroundings.

The tour, generally held year-round, then travels along a carved-out horizontal dry-cave area, past places like Fairy Ceiling, Flat Ceiling, and Lovers Leap, an extended rock finger jutting over a jumble of boulders below. After a refreshing walk through the dry part of the cave, you'll enter another wet area rich in formations, such as stalactites, stalagmites, and columns, formed by the flow of water. Here, however, you'll likely remain drier than you did while descending from New Entrance, unless hard rains have made Shower Bath Falls coming from the ceiling flow more voluminously than normal.

Ahead is Frozen Niagara, one of the cave's more spectacular formations. A set of stairs leads down to the Drapery Room, where more flowing rock formations fashion fantastical shapes, some looking like draperies from above. The last part of the tour climbs a bit, passing the deep watery pit of Crystal Lake and the tall, narrow Rainbow Dome before climbing a relatively tight passageway to emerge at the Frozen Niagara Entrance to the cave, also man-made. This spot is lower than the New Entrance, which means you net more time descending than you spent climbing.

Grand Avenue Tour

DURATION OF TOUR: 4½ hours

DISTANCE COVERED: 4 miles

TOUR SIZE LIMIT: 118

DIFFICULTY: Moderate to difficult

AGE LIMIT: Ages 6 and up allowed

HIGHLIGHTS: Rocky Mountains, Cleaveland Avenue, Snowball Room, Boone Avenue, Thorpe's Pit, Kentucky Avenue, Mount McKinley, Grand Central Station, Frozen Niagara, Shower Bath Springs, Drapery Room

This is easily the longest of Mammoth Cave's standard tours; only the strenuous Wild Cave Tour is longer in both distance and time. At 4 miles, the Grand Avenue Tour could be classified as an underground hike. Additionally, you have the option of enjoying lunch underground, and there are two bathroom stops. Yes, they have underground bathrooms at Mammoth Cave! Cave ecology and cave formation are emphasized as you travel through different types of cave passages. And covering 4 miles gives you a broader perspective of the cave.

The tour, offered year-round, starts at the Carmichael Entrance, a man-made formation blasted open in 1920s. Descend to what is known as the Rocky Mountains. Broken rocks are piled high, giving the area its name. The tour then enters mile-long Cleaveland Avenue, a wide passageway where gypsum lines the walls in many spots. The gypsum forms photo-worthy shapes in the form of flowers.

The Batcave?

At one point Mammoth Cave served as the world's largest bat hibernation site. As recently as 1850, a biologist said of the cave's bat population: "We found countless groups of them on the ceilings . . . and it is quite safe to estimate them by millions." Since those days, however, human disturbance has all but eliminated bats from Mammoth Cave—although efforts are under way to restore these critters to this, their ancestral habitat. For more information, visit www.batcon.org.

Reach the Snowball Room at the end of Cleaveland Avenue. This is your opportunity to dine underground, as cave visitors have been doing for a long time in this room discovered by famed caver Stephen Bishop. I recommend the dining experience. When else will you be able to eat lunch in a cave? The fare is limited but good, and restrooms are available. The Grand Avenue Tour then enters Boone Avenue, which offers a narrow slot-canyon-type passage. Twist and turn in the water-carved route to reach Thorpe's Pit. Other interesting points are Aero Bridge Canyon and Jack Frost, a formation resembling an icy face.

The tour then reaches Kentucky Avenue and becomes a bit more challenging, as rockfall from the cave roof makes the trail hilly—hence the name *Kentucky Avenue*. You'll spend enough time here to pass a high point known as Mount McKinley. Kentucky Avenue finally leads to Grand Central Station and arrives at a flurry of flowstone formations, such as Frozen Niagara and the Drapery Room, as well as the Moonlight Dome and Crystal Lake, tracing the route of the New Entrance Tour. It ends on a climb to reemerge into daylight at the Frozen Niagara Entrance.

Great Onyx Tour

DURATION OF TOUR: 2¼ hours

DISTANCE COVERED: 1 mile

TOUR SIZE LIMIT: 38

DIFFICULTY: Moderate

AGE LIMIT: None

HIGHLIGHTS: Pristine cave, The Nativity, The Chandelier, The Churn, Lucy's Lily

Great Onyx Cave is *not* part of Mammoth Cave. If you take this tour, then, you can't say you've been into Mammoth Cave. Also, note that this is a lantern tour; the cave is lit by handheld lantern that some visitors carry. In my opinion this is a plus, harking back to the days before electricity when all caves were toured by lantern. And the soft glow of these lights on formations adds to the ambience of the tour.

Great Onyx Cave was discovered by L. P. Edwards in the early 20th century and opened in 1915. The owners built a hotel and other amenities in the immediate area, but they were very careful in their care for the cave, leaving it in pristine shape. Most of the delicate formations are intact. This cave and area of the park was acquired by the Park Service in 1960 for $325,000. The tour travels 0.5 mile into Great Onyx Cave and returns 0.5 mile out, though 3.5 miles of the cave have been mapped. So far the cave is not connected to Mammoth Cave. A 4-mile bus ride leads along Flint Ridge Road to Great Onyx Cave entrance. Along the way you'll learn about life around Mammoth Cave before it was a national park.

The tour enters the stone entrance of Great Onyx Cave. After entering the narrow, wet initial passage, you will soon notice the fine shape of the cave. It opens into a wider, long passage, formed by underground rivers of long ago. Along the way look for formations such as The Nativity, which looks like a

Lantern light reflects on a park ranger as he leads a lantern tour, which harkens back to the cave tours of the 1800s.

Christmas scene featuring Mary holding Jesus. The lantern light really bumps this scene up. Other interesting formations are The Chandelier and The Churn. Ahead, sparkling gypsum glitters on the walls, enhancing the normally nonreflective limestone. Special gypsum formations, such as Lucy's Lily, show that gypsum can do more than sparkle.

On the way out you will see formations known as helictites. These dripstone formations must be seen to be believed. Some are very delicate and seem to grow every which way, looping in and around themselves, defying gravity. Their delicacy—which L. P. Edwards and his daughter Lucy worked so hard to preserve—makes them special. While underground, you will also learn about the Edwardses' historical tour operation, from marketing Great Onyx Cave to disputes over the ownership of this underground treasure. Exit the same place as you enter.

Historic Tour

DURATION OF TOUR: 2 hours

DISTANCE COVERED: 2 miles

TOUR SIZE LIMIT: 120

DIFFICULTY: Moderate to strenuous

AGE LIMIT: None

HIGHLIGHTS: Historic Entrance, saltpeter mine, Sidesaddle Pit, Bottomless Pit, Fat Man's Misery, River Hall, Sparks Avenue, Mammoth Dome, Ruins of Karnak

One of Mammoth's better guided tours, this is a good tour to take if you only have time for one. It offers many cave highlights and travels through passages large and small, giving tourists a good taste of the overall Mammoth experience. Part of the reason for the name *Historic Tour* is that it follows tour routes that visitors have been tracing for nearly 200 years. This tour is offered year-round.

You'll begin at the visitor center, heading down to the Historic Entrance to Mammoth Cave. There your group will gather at the saltpeter mine to learn how these operations turned the cave into the destination it is today. The tour then heads down Broadway, also known as the Main Cave, to reach the Giant's Coffin. At this point you'll leave behind the wide and open passages and turn down more narrow ways. Ahead, you'll span the Bottomless Pit, where cave

An Account of a Trip through Mammoth Cave

Some years ago, in company with an agreeable party, I spent a long summer day in exploring the Mammoth Cave in Kentucky. . . . I lost the light of one day. I saw high domes, and bottomless pits; heard the voice of unseen waterfalls; paddled three quarters of a mile in the deep Echo River, whose waters are peopled with the blind fish; crossed the streams "Lethe" and "Styx"; plied with music and guns the echoes in these alarming galleries; saw every form of stalagmite and stalactite in the sculptured and fretted chambers,— icicle, orange-flower, acanthus, grapes, and snowball. . . .

The mysteries and scenery of the cave had the same dignity that belongs to all natural objects, and which shames the fine things to which we foppishly compare them.

—Ralph Waldo Emerson
From the essay "Illusions," in *Conduct of Life*

explorer Stephen Bishop first crossed on a cedar log laid over the depths. The crowds enjoy Tall Man's Misery and Fat Man's Misery, where parades of tourists have rendered the limestone smooth in places from years of squeezing through this narrow yet fun area. The group will gather again at River Hall, named for its site near the River Styx. Here the tour reaches its lowest point, nearly 300 feet below the surface. The grand finale is the impressive Mammoth Dome, formed by the draining of Mammoth Sink on the surface. This is one of the highest water-carved areas on the cave tours. The columns of the Ruins of Karnak can be seen here as well. Added features are flowstone formations.

Since you are well down in the cave, you must go up. The tour now climbs a long set of stairs up Mammoth Dome that are an engineering feat in their own right, and will leave some people huffing and well warmed up even in the fifty-four-degree underground. After the climb, the tour returns to the Rotunda then exits the Historic Entrance via Audubon Avenue.

The entire tour is lit. The footing varies from concrete trails, to wooden walkways, to dirt trails that travel narrow passages and may make claustrophobics feel uncomfortable. Some extended stooping is required in sections, and the stairs that climb Mammoth Dome will challenge those out of shape. Moreover, there is every bit of 2 miles of walking. However, all the above should not discourage average cave visitors from this tour.

Introduction to Caving Tour

DURATION OF TOUR: 3½ hours
DISTANCE COVERED: 1.25 miles
TOUR SIZE LIMIT: 20
DIFFICULTY: Moderate to strenuous
AGE LIMIT: Ages 10 and up allowed
HIGHLIGHTS: Caving basics, cave exploration, natural cave environments

This is the second most challenging tour at Mammoth Cave. It is designed for those who want to go beyond the maintained cave trails available and get down and dirty, crawling, climbing, scrambling. Those with the moxie to take this tour will literally get their feet wet. Two experienced and knowledgeable cavers, park rangers who know not only caving but also Mammoth Cave and its human and natural history, will initiate the willing into the world of spelunking. The tour is offered year-round on weekends, and also on weekdays during summer.

Claustrophobics should stay away from this tour, as rangers will lead novices through tight spaces on seemingly long crawls over dirt and rock passages with barely enough space for an average-size person to fit. Speaking of tight spaces, this tour has restrictions. For starters, no one with a girth of more than 42 inches is allowed. Also, all cavers must be 10 years of age and up.

A miner's helmet, headlamp, and knee pads are provided to cavers. Gloves are recommended.

Mammoth Discovery Tour

DURATION OF TOUR: 1¼ hours
DISTANCE COVERED: 0.75 mile
TOUR SIZE LIMIT: None
DIFFICULTY: Easy
AGE LIMIT: None
HIGHLIGHTS: Cave visitors old and new, Historic Entrance, Great Rotunda, saltpeter mining, Indian artifacts

This tour is offered during summer to handle the crowds who want a quick overview of the cave without committing a lot of time. It's also the only cave tour that can't be reserved. On weekends the tour is unguided, but rangers are stationed at strategic and interesting locales. During summer weekdays this tour is guided. I recommend the guided tour over the unguided.

On guided tours the group assembles outside the visitor center and walks down to the Historic Entrance. After entering the cave, you'll learn about how the Houchins Narrows was named, then reassemble in the Great Rotunda, site of the saltpeter-mining operation that helped the United States win the War of 1812. The operation, still well preserved where it lies, is detailed. From here, you'll travel beyond the Rotunda down Audubon Avenue, passing a display of Indian artifacts. Speaking of aboriginals, much of the tour is devoted to the cave wanderings of those pre-Columbians who came into the cave and left their imprints, literally, but no written record; historians can only theorize on the whys of the past. Finally, the tour continues a short way beyond the Indian artifacts then turns around and backtracks to the Historic Entrance and on to the visitor center.

On the unguided tours, you'll make their way along the same route and can look around at your pleasure, reading the interpretive signs and asking questions of the rangers, who stand posted at the most interesting sights.

Almost everyone can handle the physical demands of this tour. The hardest part may be the 0.125-mile downhill walk from the visitor center to the Historic Entrance. The tour travels over smooth human-made surfaces nearly the entire trip, keeping the footing user-friendly.

River Styx Cave Tour

DURATION OF TOUR: 2½ hours

DISTANCE COVERED: 2.5 miles

TOUR SIZE LIMIT: 60

DIFFICULTY: Moderate to strenuous

AGE LIMIT: None

HIGHLIGHTS: Historic Entrance, saltpeter mine, Sidesaddle Pit, Bottomless Pit, Fat Man's Misery, Tall Man's Misery, River Hall, Dead Sea, River Styx, Lake Lethe, Sparks Avenue, Mammoth Dome, Ruins of Karnak

This is the only tour that goes all the way to the lowest of Mammoth Cave's five levels; only on this deepest level can you see some of the larger underground water features. It also travels the other levels of the cave, spotlighting geological history that includes explanations of how both the cave itself and some of its specific geological features came to be. Fear not, science-phobics, for the lessons here are described in terms everyone can understand. The tour generally follows the route of the Historic Tour, but with a different informational

*The River Styx Cave Tour begins at the visitor center, then heads into the
Historic Entrance.*

emphasis. Heading through wide rooms and narrow passageways, the walk is a real delight.

You'll begin at the visitor center, then head down to the Historic Entrance to Mammoth Cave. From there the group gathers at the Rotunda to learn the geological reasons this large room came to be. From the Rotunda, you'll cruise along Broadway to reach the Giant's Coffin and learn how it came to rest on the floor of the cave.

Now the tour changes venues and heads down Dante's Passage, then reaches the Bottomless Pit. A long walk through Fat Man's Misery and Tall Man's Misery is interesting and fun for all. At River Hall you'll take a side trip down to level five of the cave, where the water features are located. The Dead Sea is first on the lineup, and you will be surprised at the color of the water. Farther on, the trail passes the River Styx before approaching Lake Lethe and reaching the lowest point of any cave tour, 340 feet below the surface. The role of water in making the cave, and how the cave is currently being created even as you explore, is explained. You'll then return to River Hall and begin the climb up to Mammoth Dome, which also has some flowstone formations. To exit the cave, you'll climb the infamous flights of stairs to the top of Mammoth Dome before returning to the surface via Audubon Avenue.

Lighting is provided along the entire tour, and much of it follows smooth human-made surfaces, but there are narrow passageways such as Fat Man's Misery and Tall Man's Misery, which especially delight the kids. However, if you want to learn the whys and hows of Mammoth Cave's formation, this is the tour for you.

Star Chamber Tour

DURATION OF TOUR: 2½ hours

DISTANCE COVERED: 1.75 miles

TOUR SIZE LIMIT: 40

DIFFICULTY: Easy to moderate

AGE LIMIT: Ages 6 and up allowed

HIGHLIGHTS: Historic Entrance, Great Rotunda, saltpeter-mining operations, Broadway Avenue, Methodist Church, Booth's Amphitheater, Giant's Coffin, underground hospital, Star Chamber, Gothic Avenue, Signature Hall, the Bridal Altar

This evening Mammoth Cave journey follows one of the earliest tour routes. You can retrace footsteps of those who toured America's second oldest attraction over the past two centuries. Tour takers ages six and up leave the visitor center

Ralph Waldo Emerson on the Star Chamber

. . . the best thing which the cave had to offer was an illusion. On arriving at what is called the "Star-Chamber," our lamps were taken from us by the guide, and extinguished or put aside, and, on looking upwards, I saw or seemed to see the night heaven thick with stars glimmering more or less brightly over our heads, and even what seemed a comet flaming among them. . . . Some crystal specks in the black ceiling high overhead, reflecting the light of a half-hid lamp, yielded this magnificent effect.

I own, I did not like the cave so well for eking out its sublimities with this theatrical trick. But I have had many experiences like it, before and since; and we must be content to be pleased without too curiously analyzing the occasions. Our conversation with Nature is not just what it seems.

—From the essay "Illusions," in *Conduct of Life*

and walk to the Historic Entrance. Enter the cave through the opening used for millennia via Houchins Narrows to reach the Great Rotunda, one of the largest rooms at Mammoth Cave.

The Great Rotunda was site of the saltpeter-mining operations that helped the United States thwart Great Britain in the War of 1812. The works are still preserved after two centuries. This is but one of the highlights of cave history here. You also get to see the hand of mankind within the cave, from the earliest aboriginals who lit their way with cane torches, not always making it back out. Learn about the cave explorers of the early 1800s and the people who followed this same route after it became a tourist destination. Notable celebrities and other characters who toured the cave are anecdotally recalled. The formation of the cave is detailed as well.

This tour's combination of natural and human history within the cave makes for good stories of life underground, from the tuberculosis hospital of Dr. John Croghan, to the preachers who sermonized atop the rock pillar of the Methodist Church, to the first couple who got married at the interesting formation that is the Bridal Altar. At the Star Chamber you can hear Ralph Waldo Emerson's impressions of the cave and learn how stars came to be at the top of the cave. At Signature Hall, see where many early tourists marked their names in candle smoke. Countless others scratched their names upon the walls. Still others built monuments of stone with Mammoth Cave rocks. Such was the state of Mammoth Cave before it became a national park. And when you leave the cave, darkness will have fallen, and the stars from the sky will guide you back to the visitor center.

Frozen Niagara Tour

DURATION OF TOUR: 1¼ hours

DISTANCE COVERED: 0.25 mile

TOUR SIZE LIMIT: 39

DIFFICULTY: Easy

AGE LIMIT: None

HIGHLIGHTS: Crystal Lake, Frozen Niagara, Drapery Room, Shower Bath Spring

This is an introductory tour designed for the older or younger visitors and those who have difficulty walking, as well as those who want a short overview

Park enthusiasts entering Mammoth Cave at the Frozen Niagara Entrance.

of the cave or aren't sure they like caves enough to commit to an extended tour. It's offered year-round. President Ronald Reagan took this tour when he visited Mammoth Cave National Park in the 1980s. You'll take a 4-mile bus ride from the visitor center to the Frozen Niagara Entrance—a man-made cave access. From here you're led into the cave by a ranger, and travel a narrow walkway that requires some stooping. You'll pass flowing formations before coming to Crystal Lake, a body of water far below on which old-time cave tourists used to ride a boat.

The tour then arrives at Frozen Niagara, the flowstone formation that is the highlight of the trip. The flowstone resembles a frozen waterfall from top to bottom. Beyond, the *real* waterfall of Shower Bath Spring drops through the cave ceiling, splashing onto the cave floor below. This moving waterfall sheds light on the formation of Mammoth Cave.

Now you'll descend a set of stairs, optional for those who are unable or unwilling to take them, to the Drapery Room. Here, wide flowing sheets of stone and other fascinating features descend from the roof of the room above you. You are a quarter mile back into the cave. The tour then backs out of the Drapery Room and retraces the path to the Frozen Niagara Entrance. You'll see even more cave features on the return trip, followed by the bus ride back to the visitor center.

Trog Tour

DURATION OF TOUR: 2¼ hours

DISTANCE COVERED: 1 mile

TOUR SIZE LIMIT: 12

DIFFICULTY: Moderate to difficult

AGE LIMIT: Ages 8–12 allowed

HIGHLIGHTS: Worm Hole, Rambo Crawl, Duck Room, Historic Entrance, Rotunda, Giant's Coffin

This tour is for kids only, ages eight through twelve; no adults are allowed. It can be described as an introduction to caving tour for kids. Emphasis is on safe caving and working together. The group is small, twelve members, and has two guides, which personalizes the trip. Kids have a blast on this tour and are vocal about their excitement, successes, and fears underground.

First, the children gather with their parents as the guides suit up the young spelunkers with helmets, lights, and knee pads, and then give a talk on what to expect while underground. The parents stay aboveground while the group enters the Historic Entrance and heads toward the Giant's Coffin. There the real fun begins: Kids leave developed trails and enter Ganter Avenue, where they encounter names and artifacts from long-ago cave tours before they get down and dirty, crawling through passages even narrower than those on the Wild Cave Tour. The Worm Hole, a route that gradually narrows to a slit of a passage, is a big hit with the kids. Next comes the Rambo Crawl, a long belly-and-arm creep that leads to the Duck Room, so named for a rock formation resembling the bird. The tour makes its way back to Ganter Avenue and exits via the Historic Entrance.

Parents can expect their children to get quite dirty. It's caving, after all. Children should wear long pants and a long-sleeved shirt. Boots are the preferred footwear, though tennis shoes are acceptable. This tour is a summertime favorite and sells out constantly. Reservations are highly recommended.

Violet City Lantern Tour

DURATION OF TOUR: 3 hours

DISTANCE COVERED: 3 miles

TOUR SIZE LIMIT: 58

DIFFICULTY: Moderate to strenuous

AGE LIMIT: Ages 6 and up allowed

HIGHLIGHTS: Historic Entrance, The Cataracts, Mummy Ledge, Chief City, Kamper Hall, Violet City

This is one of my favorite tours. It combines cave history, from early visitors to early tourists and guides, with traveling by the light of a handheld lantern just like the tours of old. At first it travels through the most historically toured section of Mammoth Cave; it then continues into a part of the cave that is less used in this time. Here you can visit the largest room in the cave, Chief City, and see Mummy Ledge where celebrated "Lost John"—an aboriginal cave visitor—was found. The end of the tour passes through Kamper Hall and the tour's namesake, Violet City, which has eye-catching flowstone formations.

The tour is open to everyone ages six and older, but be aware that the trip travels 3 miles and progresses from leveled walkways with handrails, to leveled hard-surface trails, to relatively uneven dirt trails that have a surprising amount of ups and downs, especially toward the end. That said, the tour makes many rest stops, including breaks where benches are available, such as the Star Chamber. Also note that ten lanterns are shared by up to thirty-eight visitors, making for a limited amount of light by which to walk. The lanterns are carried by tour takers; those without lanterns have to buddy up.

Dramatic lighting illuminates the cave walls and walkway of Broadway Boardwalk.

Remnant artifacts and cave art from thousands of years ago as well as those of the American period are pointed out as you travel Broadway Avenue and what was once known as the Main Cave. See the old tuberculosis hospital ruins and the large Wright's Rotunda, just one of many natural features highlighted. The Cataracts, a high, slender, and delicate waterfall, adds a watery aspect to the tour, especially when it's lighted from the bottom up. It is beyond The Cataracts that the going gets a little more challenging, but the effort is worth it. This is the only tour that heads to Chief City, the largest single room in the entire cave system. Learn how cave explorers pushed through to Kamper Hall, which opens into Elizabeth Dome, and the stalactites and stalagmites that make a flashy ending in Violet City. The tour leaves the cave via the man-made Violet City Entrance, where a bus awaits to return you to the visitor center.

Wild Cave Tour

DURATION OF TOUR: 6½ hours

DISTANCE COVERED: 4 miles

TOUR SIZE LIMIT: 12

DIFFICULTY: Very strenuous

AGE LIMIT: Ages 16 and up allowed

HIGHLIGHTS: Safe caving techniques, environmental concerns, cave exploration past and present, working together, Carmichael Entrance, Cleaveland Avenue, Split Rock, Snowball Room, Boone Avenue, Frozen Niagara, and many tight and small passageways off the above areas

This is the most challenging cave tour open to the public. Do not attempt this tour unless you are physically fit and mentally ready to be underground for nearly an entire day, climbing, crawling on your belly over mud and dirt, squeezing into tight holes that it seems no human should travel through, by only the lights you and your fellow cavers bring. The tour is open year-round on weekends and also during summer weekdays.

The rewards are many. First, you will get to experience what it's like for modern-day cave explorers to wind their way into the labyrinth of passages that honeycomb beneath the surface of this national park. You will see how the tiniest of openings can lead to fascinating sights.

Parts of the tour travel over established trails connecting one wild part of the cave to another. Here you'll get a chance to absorb the sights around without having to focus on simply getting through the cave. One part of the tour leads to the Snowball Room, where you can eat lunch belowground and have a restroom break.

You'll not only crawl through long dirt-, rock-, water-, and mud-lined passages, but also walk along ledges, sometimes doing what's known as canyoneering, with legs straddled over a knife-like chasm below. At other times you'll slide over smooth rocks on your backside, or use handholds to scale piles of rock known as "breakdown." Though the element of danger is present on this tour, the well-trained guides inform and demonstrate the above cave moves and more to the small group and help everyone through the toughest parts, where guides are situated in safety positions.

Other parts of the tour include extended walks through long, narrow, but tall canyon-like passages that have uneven footing and rocks jutting out from the sides. Sometimes the roof overhead is low; you'll have to walk in a bent-over position for quite some time. The exact route of each cave tour varies, depending on the guides and the desires and abilities of participants.

To Lunch or Not to Lunch?

The Wild Cave Tour's lunch option, for which there is an additional fee, is well worth it. Not only does it offer the unique experience of eating tasty food underground—it also saves you the hassle of toting your lunch with you. I was very happy to have my hands and body free of a pack, while fellow cavers who chose to tote their own food began to grumble as we entered each challenging section.

Other Nearby Caves

No doubt about it, Mammoth Cave is the granddaddy of caves in south-central Kentucky. Still, this *is* cave country, so it's no surprise that many other cave attractions lie beneath the scenic rolling farmland of the area. Here are some of the cave offerings you'll find nearby:

Diamond Caverns

This cave attraction, between Park City and Mammoth Cave, has offered cave tours for a century and a half. It has thousands of stalactites, stalagmites, and flowstone deposits. Guided tours run year-round. For more information, visit www.diamondcaverns.com.

Hidden River Cave

A subterranean river is the central feature of this cave in Horse Cave, Kentucky. The entrance is quite large. Tours explore a hydroelectric system used long ago, and explain groundwater conservation. The American Cave Museum is also part of this attraction and is included in the admission price. For more information, visit www.cavern.org/hrc/hrchome.php.

Kentucky Caverns

Also located in Horse Cave, Kentucky Caverns has cave formations both large and small. Guided tours elaborate on both the natural and historical aspects of the cave. The cave here is but part of the appeal: The destination also offers aboveground fun at Kentucky Down Under, where you can interact with critters. For more information, visit www.kdu.com.

Lost River Cave

Located near the town of Bowling Green, Lost River Cave has been inhabited by many over the years. You can learn about cave history—it once housed a 1930s nightclub where cave visitors danced the night away to a band—and take cave boat tours. Aboveground attractions include nature trails and a butterfly house. For more information, visit www.lostrivercave.com.

Outlaw Cave

This cave in Cave City got its name from sheltering old-time outlaws such as Jesse James. It offers a forty-five-minute tour of cave formations. Aboveground attractions include horseback riding. For more information, visit www.kentucky actionpark.com.

Crystal Onyx Cave

Located in Cave City, the Crystal Onyx Cave is noted for the prehistoric human remains discovered in its vertical shafts. Archaeologists believe native Americans used the site as a burial ground more than 3,000 years ago. Today visitors can take guided tours of this working archaeological site and view the blind cave crayfish, the rimstone dams, and other rare formations. The human remains are not available for viewing. Aboveground the cave offers a scenic wooded campground for tents and RVs. For more information on tours or to book a campsite, visit www.crystalonyxcave.com.

Exploring Aboveground: The Trails

Mammoth Cave National Park has many interpretive trails. Most are short and fun to walk; all are designed to display and inform visitors about the unique natural beauty that the park offers. The vast majority of interpretive trails are concentrated between the visitor center and the Green River, in the general vicinity of the park accommodations and cave tour areas, allowing you to easily incorporate an aboveground stroll with your visit.

These interpretive trails add much to your understanding of how Mammoth Cave was formed and the relationship between the land and water above and the cave below. Furthermore, the trails tell of the interaction between humans and the Mammoth Cave through history. Before or after your cave tours, a walk on some of these paths will complete your picture of this park.

Mammoth Cave National Park's backcountry trails lie on the north side of the Green River. They're popular with hikers and equestrians; one trail is also open to mountain bikers. The network includes more than 50 miles of paths marked with blue metal blazes. Spur trails, such as those to backcountry campsites, are marked with orange metal blazes. Parking and access to the backcountry trails can be found at the following trailheads: Temple Hill, First

Backcountry Horse Etiquette

If you're traveling with your horse, don't tie it to trees at trail intersections and campsites; use the provided hitching posts. Otherwise, always hitch your horse at least 100 feet from designated campsites, trails, or water sources. When hikers and horses encounter each other, the horses should slow down; hikers should slip over to the downside of the trail until the horse passes. Another tip: Those without horses can rent them at Double J Stables located just outside the park. For more information see page 130.

Creek, Lincoln, Good Spring Church, and Maple Springs (see the hiker icons on the park overview map).

Interestingly, this whole area was added to the original proposal for Mammoth Cave National Park in the 1920s. At the time, most national parks were *big*; local park proponents suggested adding this land simply to increase the area's chances of reaching national park status. They succeeded, and in more ways than one: Their move not only added territory to the park, but also protected and made available a large swath of south-central Kentucky woodlands for backcountry trekkers.

Backcountry Rules and Regulations

A free backcountry permit is required for overnight stays in the backcountry. Permits are available at the information desk in the visitor center. Permits are not required for day hiking or riding, but visitors should register at trailhead registers. Overnight campers must stay at one of the twelve established backcountry campsites.

The Sal Hollow Trail is open to mountain bikers and hikers only. All other backcountry trails are open to hikers and equestrians, with the exception of some short spur trails leading from the main trails to backcountry campsites.

How to Use the Trails Information

At the top of each trail description is an at-a-glance listing that provides quick access to pertinent trail information. Here's a sample:

McCoy Hollow Trail
>**Type:** Foot and horse
>**Difficulty:** Moderate to difficult
>**Length:** 5.7 miles one-way

Mammoth Cave National Park Trail Finder Table

Trail Name	Type	Difficulty	Length (one-way)	Use	Condition
Visitor Center Area					
Interpretive Trails					
Campground Trail	F	E	0.5	M–H	G
Dixon Cave Trail	F	E	0.3	M–H	G
Echo River Springs Trail	F	E	1.1	M	G
Green River Bluffs Trail	F	E–M	1.1	M	G
Heritage Trail	F, AA	E	0.5	H	G
Mammoth Dome Sink Trail	F	E–M	1.1	M	G
River Styx Spring Trail	F	E–M	0.6	M–H	G
Other Interpretive Trails					
Cedar Sink Trail	F	M	1.1	M	G
Sand Cave Trail	F, AA	E	0.1	M	E
Sloans Crossing Pond Walk	F, AA	E	0.4 (loop)	M	E
Turnhole Bend Nature Trail	F	E	0.5 (loop)	L	G
Backcountry Trails					
Blair Spring Trail	F, E	E	1.2	M	G
Buffalo Trail	F, E	E	2.8	M	G
Collie Ridge Trail	F, E	E	3.6	H	F–G
First Creek Trail	F, E	M	6.4	M	F–G
Good Spring Loop Trail	F, E	M	7.6 (loop)	H	F–G
McCoy Hollow Trail	F, E	D	5.7	M	F–G
Raymer Hollow Trail	F, E	M–D	5.3	M	F–G
Sal Hollow Trail	F, B	M–D	8.1	M–H	G
Turnhole Bend Trail	F, E	E–M	2.5	M–H	F–G
Wet Prong of Buffalo Loop Trail	F, E	E–M	5.2 (loop)	M–H	F–G
Wet Prong–McCoy Hollow Connector Trail	F, E	E–M	0.5	M–H	F–G
White Oak Trail	F, E	M	2.5	L	G–E
Bicycle Trails					
Headquarters Campground Bike Trail	F, B	E	1	M–H	E
Mammoth Cave Railroad Bike and Hike Trail	F, B	M	4.5	M	E

Key

Type: AA = All Access, F = Foot, B = Bicycle, E = Equestrian
Difficulty: E = Easy, M = Moderate, D = Difficult
Use: L = Low, M = Moderate, H = Heavy
Condition: F = Fair, G = Good, E = Excellent

Use: Moderate
Condition: Mostly good
Highlights: Green River bluffs, views, boulder fields, Three Springs backcountry campsite, McCoy Hollow backcountry campsite
Connections: First Creek Trail, Wet Prong–McCoy Hollow Connector Trail
Access: To find McCoy Hollow Trail from the visitor center, take Mammoth Cave Parkway south for 2.9 miles to a split in the road. Veer right onto Highway 70, Brownsville Road. Follow Brownsville Road for 9.7 miles to an intersection. Turn right here and stay with Highway 70 for 0.3 mile to reach Houchins Ferry Road. Turn right onto Houchins Ferry Road and follow it for 1.8 miles to the ferry. From the ferry, take Houchins Ferry Road 1.9 miles to the Temple Hill Trailhead.

Type tells you what kinds of travel the trail is open to—foot, horse, bicycle, or any combination. Here you can see that the McCoy Hollow Trail is open to foot and horse travel. Three of the interpretative trails are "all acccess," which means they are wheelchair-accessible. **Difficulty** is listed as easy, moderate, or difficult (or some combination); rated moderate to difficult, this particular trail has numerous ups and downs, and the footing can be troublesome in places. **Length** is of course 5.7 miles one-way. Note that many of the trails, short or long, connect to other trails. Trails in the text are generally described as "one-way," "loop," or "out-and-back." "One-way" means that you will connect with other trails and, therefore, have the option of extending your trip or returning the way you came—so expect to add to this initial mileage. "Loop" indicates that the trail is configured as a loop and includes the total mileage. "Out-and-back" means you have no choice but to return the way you came; in the Trail Finder Table you will see the one-way mileage listed for these trails, however, for your convenience later in this book this one-way mileage has been doubled to provide the total mileage.

Use, defined as how frequently the path is traveled, can be listed in this book as low, moderate, or heavy. **Condition** offers some details on the state of the walkway. **Highlights** of each trail are listed as well—in this case the bluffs of the Green River, views, boulder fields, and backcountry campsites along the way. **Connections** tells you what other trails connect to this one. The McCoy Hollow Trail connects to the First Creek and Wet Prong–McCoy Hollow Connector Trails. This way you can look up these other trails to create loops or extended one-way trips. **Access** provides specific directions to the trailhead.

Following the at-a-glance information is a running narrative of the trail, which notes trail junctions, stream crossings, and trailside features along with their distance from the trailhead. This helps keep you apprised of your where-abouts and ensures that you don't miss the features noted. Using the narrative, you can come up with a short loop, a ride, a hike, or a backpack trip of your own making.

Interpretive Trails in the Visitor Center Area

Campground Trail

TYPE: Foot

DIFFICULTY: Easy

LENGTH: 0.5 mile one-way

USE: Moderate to heavy

CONDITION: Good

HIGHLIGHTS: Connects campground to Mammoth Dome Sink Trail

CONNECTIONS: Mammoth Dome Sink Trail

ACCESS: The Campground Trail starts near campsite 107, in the 92–111 loop of the Headquarters Campground.

This short path leaves near campsite 107, which is in the D Loop of the campground. Take the path downhill over one bridge; where one trail continues ahead toward the park amphitheater, turn left onto an old roadbed. The Campground Trail heads along this roadbed through level land, passing the Campfire Circle, a small amphitheater. Keep west on the old roadbed as the flat narrows; the trail then makes a hard left downhill, while an unmaintained trail keeps forward. Descend then make a hard right, as the roadbed you have been following continues toward Green River Ferry Road. Enter a world of cedar trees shading rock outcrops, a scenic area, before meeting the Mammoth Dome Sink Trail near White's Cave.

Dixon Cave Trail

TYPE: Foot

DIFFICULTY: Easy

LENGTH: 0.3 mile one-way

USE: Moderate to heavy

CONDITION: Good

HIGHLIGHTS: Historic Entrance to Mammoth Cave, Dixon Cave

CONNECTIONS: River Styx Spring Trail, Green River Bluffs Trail

ACCESS: To find the Dixon Cave Trail from the visitor center, begin heading toward the park hotel—but immediately behind the visitor center building turn right, following signs to the Historic Entrance. Join a paved road leading down a wooded hollow and come to the Historic Entrance on your right. The Dixon Cave Trail leaves right and uphill from the entrance. The trail begins 0.2 mile from the center.

This short path begins at the Historic Entrance to Mammoth Cave and then ascends along a bluff line to pass Dixon Cave. It continues to meet the Green River Bluffs Trail near a scenic overlook. After reaching the historic Mammoth Cave entrance, veer right and uphill. Stay below a bluff line to your right. The trail opens and the path curves onto a dry ridgeline, where mountain laurels, dogwoods, and chestnut oaks thrive.

Ahead, the trail curves and reaches Dixon Cave. This cave is fenced in to keep unauthorized explorers from disturbing the habitat of the Indiana cave bat. You'll now cross a dry rocky wash before intersecting the Green River Bluffs Trail. From there the Green River Bluffs Trail leads left, downhill to the Green River, and right, past a scenic overlook and on to the Headquarters Picnic Area. Dead ahead, another short path leads to stone bluffs looking down on the Green River.

Echo River Springs Trail

TYPE: Foot

DIFFICULTY: Easy

LENGTH: 1.1 miles one-way

USE: Moderate

CONDITION: Good

HIGHLIGHTS: Echo River Springs, River Styx Spring, spring wildflowers, big trees

CONNECTIONS: Mammoth Dome Sink Trail, River Styx Spring Trail, Green River Bluffs Trail, shortcut trail between Mammoth Dome Sink and Echo River

ACCESS: To find the Echo River Springs Trail from the visitor center, take Mammoth Cave Parkway south for 0.6 mile to the first right, Green River Ferry Road. Turn right onto Green River Ferry Road and

Indiana Cave Bats

This fascinating—and endangered—bat species is centered in the Midwest. Its range extends from the western edge of the Ozark region in Oklahoma, to southern Wisconsin, east to Vermont, and as far south as northern Florida. In summer it is apparently absent south of Tennessee; in winter it is apparently absent from Michigan, Ohio, and northern Indiana, where suitable caves and mines are not found to scientists' current knowledge. About half a million individual Indiana cave bats still exist.

follow it for 1.3 miles to the Green River. The parking area is on your right; the Echo River Springs Trail starts on the side of the parking area away from the river.

Though this path starts at Green River Ferry, it is considered part of the greater network of interpretive trails emanating from the visitor center. It begins at the parking area near the *Miss Green River II* boat dock and works around the Echo River Springs, then cruises the bottomland of the Green River before reaching the River Styx Spring.

Leave the Green River Ferry parking area and head east along the Echo River, the outflow of the Echo River Springs. This area is rich in spring wildflowers. Soon you'll circle right around the boil of the Echo River Springs. Notice that upstream, above the spring, the Echo River is but a rocky, intermittent streambed. Descend along the short Echo River to reach the Green River bottomland. Moss-trunked maples, big sycamores, and other trees stand over flowers such as spring beauties. Reach a trail junction. Here a shortcut trail leads right, up to Mammoth Dome Sink Trail.

The Echo River Springs Trail ascends from the junction with the shortcut trail and passes a stone cabin on your right, an old water treatment building. Enter a cedar forest. Shagbark hickory grows among the evergreen trees here. The slope sharpens; soon you're walking a stone bluff and can look down on the River Styx Spring below. Descend a hill from the bluff above this

A trillium near the Echo River.

spring to reach a deck overlooking it, and then a trail junction in a flat beside the Green River. Here the River Styx Spring Trail leads right, uphill, for 0.6 mile to the Historic Entrance to Mammoth Cave and 0.2 mile farther to the visitor center. Ahead, the Green River Bluffs Trail leads 1.1 miles to the Headquarters Picnic Area.

Green River Bluffs Trail

TYPE: Foot

DIFFICULTY: Easy to moderate

LENGTH: 1.1 miles one-way

USE: Moderate

CONDITION: Good

HIGHLIGHTS: Views of Green River, rock bluffs, big trees

CONNECTIONS: Dixon Cave Trail, River Styx Spring Trail, Echo River Springs Trail

ACCESS: The Green River Bluffs Trail starts in the Headquarters Picnic Area, at the point where the road through the picnic area makes a loop.

This path leaves the Headquarters Picnic Area and curves into the Green River Valley, reaching a cleared overlook with a stellar view to the Green River and beyond. It then passes a spur trail that travels along bluffs before descending to the Green River itself in a bottomland forest of big trees.

Leave the Headquarters Picnic Area at the point where the picnic road makes a loop. The path leaves to your right, passing through a prototype upland hardwood forest. It then descends into a moister forest and joins the upper Green River Valley. Reach a contemplation bench and cleared view, one of the best in the park. The Green River flows below and gently curves. The valley rises sharply on the other side of the river.

Reach a trail junction. A short spur trail leads past sheer bluffs high above the river. Ahead is another junction. Here the Dixon Cave Trail leaves left 0.3 mile to the Historic Entrance of Mammoth Cave and 0.2 mile farther to the visitor center. To your right a spur trail leads to the rock bluffs and back to the Green River Bluffs Trail.

Descend by switchbacks through cedar woods. The Green River comes into view on your right. Notice Cave Island in the river. Massive sycamore trees tower overhead. Pass over a dry streamed on a bridge with old stone abutments. Reach a trail junction. Here the Echo River Springs Trail leads right to an old steamboat landing, and left (uphill) the River Styx Spring Trail leads to the historic Mammoth Cave entrance. Ahead, the Echo River Springs Trail leads along the Green River to the Echo River Springs and the Green River Ferry parking area.

Heritage Trail

TYPE: Foot, all access

DIFFICULTY: Easy

LENGTH: 0.5 mile one-way

USE: Heavy

CONDITION: Good

HIGHLIGHTS: Old Guide's Cemetery, views of Historic Entrance, Green River Valley, Sunset Point

CONNECTIONS: Mammoth Dome Sink Trail

ACCESS: To find the Heritage Trail from the visitor center, take the land bridge toward the park hotel. Just before reaching the hotel, turn right and begin following the trail that runs behind it.

This walk is easy and enlightening, once you find the trailhead. Leave the visitor center and cross the bridge toward the park hotel. The trail begins just before you reach the hotel, on your right. A boardwalk leads behind the hotel. The hollow to your right dips past the Historic Entrance to Mammoth Cave and farther down to the Green River. Leave the hotel behind and reach a deck extending into the hollow below. You can see the Historic Entrance, one of twenty-four entrances into the underworld protected by this park. This entrance is where early settlers began to explore the cave, long after indigenous peoples had roamed the darkness. An old homesite is located on the uphill side of the deck. The level spot and spring flowers mark its presence. Reach a trail junction. A path leads forward to the Old Guide's Cemetery. This is where famed cave explorer Stephen Bishop is interred, along with some tuberculosis patients who once lived in the cave, attempting to restore their health.

The Heritage Trail begins its loop. To your right it runs along a steep hill, which was rendered more open after storms in the early 2000s. Notice the abundance of beech trees on the north-facing slope. Ahead, the path opens to a vista known as Sunset Point. Here a view has been cleared into the lower Green River Valley, and also to the northeast. Views such as these show off the aboveground allure of this national park. Now the trail curves away from the bluffs and completes its loop. To your right, the Mammoth Dome Sink Trail leads 1.1 miles to the Green River Ferry parking area. The Heritage Trail backtracks to the hotel.

Massive sycamores rise above the Kentucky forest floor.

Mammoth Dome Sink Trail

TYPE: Foot

DIFFICULTY: Easy to moderate

LENGTH: 1.1 miles one-way

USE: Moderate

CONDITION: Good

HIGHLIGHTS: Mammoth Dome Sink, White's Cave, overlook

CONNECTIONS: Heritage Trail, Echo River Springs Trail, Campground Trail, shortcut trail to Echo River Springs Trail

ACCESS: The Mammoth Dome Sink Trail can be reached by walking the Heritage Trail from the visitor center or taking the Echo River Springs Trail from the Green River Ferry parking area.

The Mammoth Dome Sink Trail displays part of the relationship between above- and belowground water-flow patterns in this cave-laden park. This high-and-low path leaves Mammoth Cave Ridge from the Heritage Trail and works its way toward the Echo River Springs Trail, passing two sinks, then works around a ridgeline, also passing White's Cave. Beyond White's Cave the trail descends along rock bluffs to reach bottomland by the Echo River.

Leave the Heritage Trail and head southwest in a young forest, passing a stone cabin that hosts the park's sewage system. An interpretive display explains the park's commitment to water treatment. Soon you'll reach a spur trail leading to a contemplation bench and an overlook of the Green River. The main trail turns left here and descends below a bluff line. Notice how the waters that flow off this bluff drop into a wooded sinkhole below. Descend along the left side of the sinkhole and keep descending to reach the spur trail to Mammoth Dome Sink. Logs and debris have gathered atop this place where groundwater seeps into the cave system below. You can see the point where this water enters the cave at Mammoth Dome on two cave tours, the Historic Tour and the River Styx Cave Tour. Upstream, an intermittent streambed ends its downhill journey at Mammoth Dome Sink. Just ahead, a shortcut trail leads right down to the Echo River Springs Trail. The Mammoth Dome Sink Trail leaves the sink and curves around an unnamed ridgeline to reach White's Cave—a small opening to the left of the trail. You can look inside this cave, but it's gated.

Reach a trail junction just beyond White's Cave. Here the Campground Trail leads left 0.5 mile to Headquarters Campground, while the Mammoth Dome Sink Trail begins heading toward Echo River Springs. It angles down the hill amid cedars and oaks, curving around a dry hollow. Interestingly, the path descends by switchbacks between layers of rock shaded by cedars. The rock layers are laid out almost like steps. Reach the junction with the Echo River Springs Trail. At this point the Echo River Springs Trail leads a short distance left around the Echo Springs and to the Green River Ferry parking area. To the right, the Echo River Springs Trail cruises down the Echo River Springs Branch, then along bottomland to reach the River Styx Spring Trail.

River Styx Spring Trail

TYPE: Foot

DIFFICULTY: Easy to moderate

LENGTH: 0.6 mile one-way

USE: Moderate to heavy

CONDITION: Good

HIGHLIGHTS: Big trees, River Styx Spring, old ferry landing

CONNECTIONS: Dixon Cave Trail, Green River Bluffs Trail, Echo River Springs Trail

ACCESS: To find the River Styx Spring Trail from the visitor center, begin heading south on the land bridge toward the park hotel—but immediately behind the visitor center building turn right, following signs to the Historic Entrance. Join a paved road leading down a wooded hollow and come to the Historic Entrance on your right. The River Styx Spring Trail begins dead ahead on a gravel track. It is 0.2 mile from the visitor center to the trailhead.

The River Styx Spring Trail begins at Mammoth Cave's Historic Entrance and leads down to the Green River floodplain, populated with big trees. Backed against a bluff is the River Styx Spring, which emerges with a strong flow and runs to the Green River. Leave the Historic Entrance and descend a hollow on a wide gravel track. A normally dry streambed is off to your right. The hollow widens and opens onto the rich Green River floodplain. Massive sycamore trees extend skyward, flanked by cane and beech and maple. This cane was collected and used by cave-exploring aboriginals for lighting when they went underground thousands of years ago. They bound the reeds, carrying multiple bundles, and lit each bundle as they proceeded into the cave. Each bundle lasted around forty-five minutes.

Reach a trail junction. To your left, the Echo River Springs Trail leads 1.1 miles to Green River Ferry, and a boardwalk leads to the River Styx Spring. To your right, the Green River Bluffs Trail leads 1.1 miles to the Headquarters Picnic Area. Ahead, the River Styx Spring Trail continues in bottomland and

The Stygian Spring

The boardwalk leading to the River Styx Spring is well worth visiting. The spring upwelling is backed against a steep bluff. From the point of its emergence, the water flows as a creek for 50 yards or so into the Green River.

ends at the confluence of the River Styx, the outflow of the River Styx Spring, and the Green River. The old steamboat landing was an unloading point for passengers and supplies for early cave tourists.

Other Park Interpretive Trails

Cedar Sink Trail

TYPE: Foot

DIFFICULTY: Moderate

LENGTH: 2.2 miles out-and-back

USE: Moderate

CONDITION: Good

HIGHLIGHTS: Cedar Sink, spring wildflowers

CONNECTIONS: None

ACCESS: To find the Cedar Sink Trail from the visitor center, follow Mammoth Cave Parkway for 2.9 miles to an intersection. Veer right onto Brownsville Road, Highway 70. Stay with Highway 70 for 3.3 miles, then turn left onto Cedar Sink Road and follow it 0.4 mile to the trailhead, on your left.

This trail is renowned for its spring wildflowers as well as its massive sinkholes—some of the biggest in an area known as the "Land of 10,000 Sinks." The path mostly descends to reach the sink, passing old roads and possible homesites in an area that has returned to a more natural state. Leave Cedar Sink Road on a gravel path and immediately enter a cedar forest. Soon you'll span a wooden bridge over a dry streambed. Keep southerly on a hillside that rises to your right. The trail levels off, then makes a sudden drop to the left and turns right to enter a flat. This bottomland is lush. Bisect the flat then turn right, joining an old roadbed. This roadbed climbs to turn left in an area of big beech trees surrounding a level area that may once have been a homesite. The land around here was certainly manipulated at one time.

Dutchman's breeches thrive in Cedar Sink.

Now the path passes a less obvious roadbed then comes to an observation deck. This deck overlooks a short stream below. Just below you, water emerges from the base of the base of the bluff and flows a short distance to the actual sink, where logs have congregated atop a pool, and disappears underground. The trail works its way farther down the sink to reach a bluff line, which is negotiated by metal stairs. You are now entering the rich wildflower area, where Dutchman's breeches, trilliums, and other flowers thrive. The official trail crosses the bottomland of the sink area and spans a bridge to reach another observation deck. Here you can look down upon the main sink.

Sand Cave Trail

TYPE: Foot, all access

DIFFICULTY: Easy

LENGTH: 0.2 mile out-and-back

USE: Moderate

CONDITION: Excellent

HIGHLIGHTS: Sand Cave

CONNECTIONS: None

ACCESS: To find the Sand Cave Trail from the visitor center, take Mammoth Cave Parkway south for 1.3 miles. Turn left onto Cave City Road and follow it for 2.8 miles to the Sand Cave Trail parking area, on your left.

This short trail follows a boardwalk through woods its entire length to reach Sand Cave. It's an ideal way for disabled people to experience a cedar forest and get a glimpse of Sand Cave. An incident at Sand Cave was partially responsible for the establishment of Mammoth Cave National Park. In 1925 cave explorer Floyd Collins was trapped in this cave. Rescuers spent more than two weeks attempting to rescue him while the nation intently followed the story. Although the efforts failed, the Mammoth Cave area received extensive publicity, which aided in its establishment as a national park.

This boardwalk travels through cedar woods then descends slightly to reach a bluff above Sand Cave. Here, the drip of water into the cave signals your arrival. Take note that the actual passageway for the cave opening was closed and gated before Mammoth Cave National Park was established. You can, however, look into the darkness of the cave opening and contemplate the past this cave has seen. In summer the park offers a ranger-led walk on this trail known as Sand Cave Almanac. Check the visitor center for dates and times.

The Sand Cave Trail leads to the site of one of America's most stirring events of the 1920s.

Sloans Crossing Pond Walk

TYPE: Foot, all access

DIFFICULTY: Easy

LENGTH: 0.4-mile loop

USE: Moderate

CONDITION: Excellent

HIGHLIGHTS: Views of pond, wheelchair-accessible trail

CONNECTIONS: None

ACCESS: The boardwalk can be reached from the visitor center by taking the Mammoth Cave Parkway south for 2.9 miles. Stay left here, still on

Mammoth Cave Parkway; Sloans Crossing Pond Walk is immediately on your right.

The interrelationship between land and water at Mammoth Cave National Park results in limited natural surface water and a few stillwater ponds. The one you'll visit on this trail, Sloans Crossing Pond, was perhaps a sink that at one time held some water. During the time when the park was settled, however, the sink was dammed and the water level rose. The result is this quiet stillwater ecosystem where frogs croak and birds congregate.

This trail is one of the few paths in the park offering surface water views and habitat. A deck extends into the water at the trailhead, allowing you to survey Sloans Pond. The main boardwalk begins to circle the pond in a transitional forest, where dry ridgetop trees such as oak, dogwood, and cedar commingle with more moisture-loving species like tulip trees along the pond's edge. Pass a viewing bench then keep circling to cross the pond's outlet. A second deck extends into the water before the boardwalk completes its loop around Sloans Pond.

Turnhole Bend Nature Trail

TYPE: Foot

DIFFICULTY: Easy

LENGTH: 0.5-mile loop

USE: Low

CONDITION: Good

HIGHLIGHTS: Views of Green River, Turnhole Spring

CONNECTIONS: None

ACCESS: To find the Turnhole Bend Nature Trail from the visitor center, follow Mammoth Cave Parkway for 2.9 miles to an intersection. Veer right onto Brownsville Road, Highway 70. Stay with Highway 70 for 3.7 miles to the trailhead, on your right.

Located off the main circuit, this path deserves more attention. It offers a short loop walk and is an excellent leg stretcher, with a few hills but nothing too strenuous. Along the way it passes large sinks and a vista.

Leave the parking area and climb a few stairs to reach the loop portion of the path. Turn right and ascend a south-facing slope in oak-dominated woodland. Level off and bridge an old roadbed that now acts as a creekbed. Soon you reach a contemplation bench; the Green River Valley lies across the way. Descend into a moister environment where tulip trees grow. A wooded sink is on your right. However, a more impressive rock-rimmed sink is to your left. A short path leads to this sink. The valley opens before you, and the trail reaches an observation deck. The Green River lies far below. The lowermost part of the water is the inflow of Turnhole Spring. This is only one part of the "bend" of Turnhole Bend. It actually starts beyond the view as the river heads south, then west, then turns back north at the point you can see below.

Backcountry turtle rambles downhill.

From here, the trail ascends to join an old roadbed and climbs past the other side of the rock-rimmed sink. However, a new sink lies ahead, this time on your right. This is a large wooded sink, bordered on one side by bluffs. You are atop the ridge again. A contemplation bench overlooks the sink. The trail travels its last part beneath oaks again before completing the loop at 0.5 mile.

Hiking the Backcountry Trails

Blair Spring Trail

TYPE: Foot and horse

DIFFICULTY: Easy

LENGTH: 1.2 miles one-way

USE: Moderate

CONDITION: Good

HIGHLIGHTS: Magnolia trees, Wet Prong

CONNECTIONS: Wet Prong of Buffalo Loop Trail, Collie Ridge Trail

ACCESS: The Blair Spring Trail is an interior trail. It can be reached by heading south on the Collie Ridge Trail for 1.9 miles to its eastern terminus, or by taking the Wet Prong of Buffalo Loop Trail for 1.4 miles to the west end.

The Blair Spring Trail is an interior trail that links Collie Ridge on the east with Wet Prong Buffalo Creek to the west. It's the shortest backcountry trail in the park. There are no campsites along it.

Spring is a great time to backpack at Mammoth Cave—when the aboveground trails are alive with wildflowers.

Blair Spring Trail leaves Collie Ridge west on a dry hickory-oak slope, pocked with mountain laurel. It runs along a ridgeline before descending along a small stream. Watch as the stream flows down into a rocky sink, doing its part to carve the limestone labyrinth belowground. Continue descending beyond the sink to reach Wet Prong Buffalo Creek at 1 mile. This generally clear stream is easily crossed in times of normal flow. Just upstream lies the confluence of two forks that form Wet Prong. Beyond the crossing, the Blair Spring Trail turns left, downstream.

The Blair Spring Trail heads downstream past big-leaf magnolia trees, which thrive in moist hollows such as this. To your left, attractive Wet Prong flows over rocks and along sandbars into pools. At 1.2 miles, reach a trail junction. Here the Wet Prong of Buffalo Loop Trail leads forward, downstream, for 1.7 miles to meet the Wet Prong–McCoy Hollow Connector Trail. To your right the Wet Prong of Buffalo Loop Trail leads uphill for 1.4 miles to the First Creek Trailhead on Houchins Ferry Road.

Buffalo Trail

TYPE: Foot and horse

DIFFICULTY: Easy

LENGTH: 2.8 miles one-way

USE: Moderate

CONDITION: Good

HIGHLIGHTS: Homesites, sink

CONNECTIONS: Sal Hollow Trail, Turnhole Bend Trail, Good Spring Loop Trail

ACCESS: To find the Buffalo Trail from the visitor center, take Mammoth Cave Parkway for 0.6 mile, then turn right onto Green River Ferry Road. Follow this road for 3.4 miles to Maple Springs Road; turn left and continue 1 mile to the Maple Springs Trailhead. The Buffalo Trail can be accessed by taking the unmarked gravel track on the west side of the road next to the MAPLE SPRINGS TRAILHEAD sign, or by traveling north just a short distance farther on Maple Springs Road, turning left onto the gravel road toward Good Spring Church, and following this road 0.1 mile to the pole gate and the signed beginning of the Buffalo Trail. As of this writing the Buffalo Trail is signed BUFFALO ROAD.

The author peers into a sinkhole along the Buffalo Trail. These sinkholes are part of the relationship between land, water, and cave.

The Buffalo Trail begins at the Maple Springs Trailhead and uses old roads in its westward quest to meet the Good Spring Loop Trail, passing old homesites along the way. Toward its end, it makes quite a few twists and turns as it meanders along roads that once skirted the property lines where settlers had homes. You'll find an interesting sink on the latter half of the trail as well. The path has few elevation changes, but it does pass over a few stream branches before its end. It's primarily used as a part of a loop, in combination with either the Good Spring Loop Trail or the Sal Hollow Trail. There are no backcountry campsites along it, though the Bluffs site isn't far from its western end.

The Buffalo Trail officially starts on the far side of the pole gate at the hard right turn on the gravel road to Good Spring Church. It follows the old Buffalo Road, which was lined with homes aplenty in pre-park days. Cedar and hardwoods shade the gravel track that tacks southwesterly. Dip to a streambed. Here, and in other places, the long-used track has cut a deep bed below the land above it. The path is level more often than not. At 1.1 miles you'll intersect the Turnhole Bend Trail, which to your left heads 1.8 miles to the Turnhole Bend backcountry campsite; to your right, 0.7 mile to the Good Spring Loop Trail.

The Buffalo Trail now saddles alongside a dry limestone streambed that works down into Sal Hollow, which eventually meets the Green River. Other dry streambeds course across the trail amid tall timber. The path curves north only to make a hard left, turning westbound, at 1.6 miles. It now stays on the ridgeline to the north of Sal Hollow. Watch for a sinkhole to your left at 2.1 miles. A streambed empties into the sink. If you peer down, you can see the former roof of the sink, which collapsed from undercutting moisture as it seeped into a small fissure in the ground. Finally the weight of the rock and soil over the hole became too much to bear, causing the cave-in. Water continues eroding the rock below the sink to this day.

Beyond the sink, the Buffalo Trail makes a hard left turn, now southbound. At this point the path begins turning more often at angles until it intersects the Sal Hollow Trail at 2.8 miles. Watch carefully here—this spot can be confusing. Ahead, a closed roadbed leads forward, but the Buffalo Trail turns right on a much narrower track and soon meets the Good Spring Loop Trail and its terminus. From here, the Good Spring Loop Trail leads left 1.7 miles to Collie Ridge and right 2.4 miles to Good Spring Church.

Collie Ridge Trail

TYPE: Foot and horse

DIFFICULTY: Easy

LENGTH: 3.6 miles one-way

USE: Heavy

CONDITION: Good in some places; extremely muddy or dusty in others

HIGHLIGHTS: Good connector trail in the heart of the backcountry, Collie Ridge backcountry campsite

CONNECTIONS: Raymer Hollow Trail, Blair Spring Trail, Good Spring Loop Trail, McCoy Hollow Trail

ACCESS: To find Collie Ridge Trail from the visitor center, head south for 0.6 mile to Green River Ferry Road. Turn right and follow this road for 1.3 miles, then continue for 5.7 miles to Highway 1827. Turn left and follow Highway 1827 for 1.1 miles to Ollie Road. Turn left onto Ollie Road and proceed 0.4 mile to the Lincoln Trailhead, on your left. The trailhead has shaded parking spurs suitable for horse trailers and hikers alike.

The Collie Ridge Trail traverses a crest dividing the Wet and Dry Prongs of Buffalo Creek. It's a heavily used horse trail and even has a spur path connecting to a park-permitted equestrian outfitter. The path leaves the Lincoln Trailhead and works its way south, then southwest along an old roadbed to end not far from the Green River, where it forms one leg of an important trail junction. It has a gentle grade through most of its length, with very few steep sections. However, at times the trail can be a victim of its own popularity: Too many horses can turn it into a miry mess in places, or pound it into a dust bowl. Still, the park does conduct regular maintenance on the path, which is in good shape considering the amount of use it receives.

Leave the Lincoln Trailhead on a narrow path descending through a hardwood forest dotted with pines. Traverse a dry drainage then reach a wide roadbed at 0.3 mile. Here the blue-blazed path turns right on the track, continuing a downgrade. Saddle alongside a branch to reach a trail junction at 0.8 mile. A spur path leads left and uphill to Double J Stables, a horse rental and equestrian camp facility. (For more information, see www.doublejstables.com.)

The Collie Ridge Trail continues forward, passing over the uppermost part of "Dry" Prong—a part that may actually be flowing. Make a moderate but steady ascent from the creek, leveling out in an open area. The forest here is tall. Reach a high point at 1.3 miles. The mostly shaded path stays on cruise control, commanding the center of Collie Ridge, which slopes away on both sides.

Reach a trail junction at 1.9 miles. Here, the Blair Spring Trail leaves right and travels 1.2 miles to the Wet Prong Buffalo Trail. The Raymer Hollow Trail leaves left 5.3 miles to Maple Springs Loop Road. The Collie Ridge Trail continues forward then turns southeast, reaching the Sand Springs Cemetery at 2.1 miles. Here you'll find quite a few primitive stones serving as markers. Curve back to the southwest, making a rocky descent to a gap. As you climb out of the gap, look left below the trail for a large rock overhang, similar to those in eastern Kentucky. At 2.4 miles, intersect the Good Spring Loop Trail, which heads left for 1.7 miles to the Good Spring Church Trailhead. The Collie Ridge Trail keeps forward, now running in conjunction with the part of the Good Spring Loop Trail that runs along Collie Ridge.

The Collie Ridge Trail continues to divide the watersheds, and maintains a southwesterly direction. Homesites are prevalent along this part of the trail. Look for large trees beside the trail—these are often indicators of homesites. Open rock slabs spill over the trailbed in places. The path can be sandy in shallow gaps. The Collie Ridge Trail ends at a trail junction at 3.6 miles. Here the

McCoy Hollow Trail leaves right and travels 5.7 miles to Houchins Ferry Road, while the Good Spring Loop Trail heads left for 4.1 miles to Good Spring Church. A short spur trail leads straight ahead to the Collie Ridge backcountry campsite.

First Creek Trail

TYPE: Foot and horse

DIFFICULTY: Moderate

LENGTH: 6.4 miles one-way

USE: Moderate

CONDITION: Mostly good

HIGHLIGHTS: Nolin River, First Creek Lake, homesites, Second Creek backcountry campsite, First Creek 1 backcountry campsite, First Creek 2 backcountry campsite, spring wildflowers, unusual plant species

CONNECTIONS: Wet Prong of Buffalo Loop Trail, McCoy Hollow Trail

ACCESS: To find First Creek Trail from the visitor center, head south for 0.6 mile. Turn right onto Green River Ferry Road and follow it for 1.3 miles, then continue for 5.7 miles to Highway 1827. Turn left and follow Highway 1827 for 1.1 miles to Ollie Road. Turn left onto Ollie Road, follow it for 2.7 miles to Houchins Ferry Road, then turn left again and follow Houchins Ferry Road for 0.1 mile to reach the trailhead, on your right. The south end of the trail is 5.2 miles farther south on Houchins Ferry Road.

Fire pinks illuminate the woods along the First Creek Trail.

The First Creek Trail is a linear path with a loop in the middle. This loop circles First Creek Lake, a small body of water that adds some watery scenery to the trail. There are three backcountry campsites along the way, making overnight stays here a cinch. Two of the campsites are along the shores of First Creek Lake. The path first travels an old road then follows a ridge running westward over some rocky ground, passing a small shower-like waterfall. You'll then dip into a moist rock mini gorge where hemlocks, unusual for this region, grow. After reaching the lower Nolin River Valley, you'll turn south and come to the loop portion of the trail, where you have an option as to which way to pass around First Creek Lake. Climb a north-facing slope rich in wildflowers before working beyond massive boulders, finally reaching the Temple Hill Trailhead.

The First Creek Trail leaves First Creek Trailhead from the lower end of the teardrop-shaped parking area. The path dips to a draw that runs to the First Creek drainage, to your left (south). Pass a second branch, then climb toward the park border. Here, at a gate on the boundary line at 0.7 mile, the First Creek Trail joins old Clell Road, heading southwest, shaded by Virginia pines, dogwoods, and oaks. The trail begins to straddle the ridgeline dividing First and Second Creeks. The old road makes for easy walking as it passes a homesite on your right marked by persistent yuccas, planted by the forgotten settler who cleared this now forested country. Undulate along the ridgeline and make a turn to the right, now heading westerly. At 1.4 miles in Virginia pine, the path abruptly leaves the roadbed right, tracing a more obscure track.

At 2.5 miles you'll descend abruptly to reach a shower-like, low-flow waterfall dropping over a rock rim. The rock is carved out beneath the rim, forming a small shelter. From here the path descends further to a moist mini gorge; hemlock trees thrive in the cool, shady environment. Soon you'll turn away from the gorge and traverse a linear, sloped rock slab that proves difficult to navigate. Note the change in vegetation here, as the south-facing slope harbors mountain laurel and chestnut oaks, which enjoy drier situations than hemlock. A keen eye will also spot prickly pear cactus, another dry-site species very unusual for these parts. In just a short span the trail displays the rich biodiversity, from hemlocks to cacti, that makes this park so special above the ground as well as below.

The path joins the top of the ridge, which now becomes narrow and rocky. Steep bluffs drop off to your right, and occasional views open into Second Creek below. Notice the hemlock trees here, too, that grow just below the rock face on the north side of the ridge. Descend away from this interesting area to intersect the spur trail to Second Creek backcountry campsite at 3.1 miles. Keep descending into moister terrain beyond the spur trail. Magnolia trees grow trailside. Second Creek comes into view on your right. The hillside is steep here as the path circles the Second Creek Campsite uphill. At 3.3 miles, reach a spur trail leading right, down a bluff, to the exact point where Second Creek and the Nolin River meet.

Now the First Creek Trail turns south into the immediate Nolin River Valley. To your right is the bottomland of the river; a bluff rises to your left.

Prickly pear cacti are another example of Mammoth Cave biodiversity.

Straight-trunked tulip trees, sycamores, and maples form much of the forest. Ahead, to your right, look for piled rocks amid the woods before coming to a chimney and other metal relics marking an old homesite at 3.8 miles. Beyond the homesite, cross a streamlet with a waterfall dropping over a rock formation upstream, within sight of the trail. The path then reaches the loop portion of the First Creek Trail at 4.2 miles. Here the main trail leaves left 1 mile to circle First Creek Lake, whereas the shorter part of the loop cuts through the cedar-laden First Creek bottomland to reach First Creek 1 campsite and the outflow of First Creek from First Creek Lake, then rejoins the lake-circling portion of trail after 0.3 mile.

The main trail leaves left from the junction, beginning its circuit around the lake to cross a tributary of First Creek, then turns downstream. First Creek Lake comes intro view. But the trail turns away from the lake and begins ascending along First Creek before dropping to cross the streambed of First Creek, very likely to be dry, at 4.9 miles. Climb away from First Creek and continue around the lake, which comes into view once again. Reach the spur trail to First Creek 2 backcountry campsite at 5.2 miles. Here the spur trail leads 0.1 mile to a level area where campers have a view of the lake.

The First Creek Trail reaches the junction with the other part of the loop at 5.3 miles. The First Creek 1 backcountry campsite lies just across a bridge over the outflow of First Creek Lake. It sits beside the outflow on a low bluff near First Creek Lake. The main part of the First Creek Trail climbs south away from First Creek Lake and along a bluff line that is perhaps one of the most productive wildflower areas in the park. Celandine poppy, Jack-in-the-pulpit, and trillium are among the many species that thrive here. Keep downstream well above the Nolin River, then ascend along a drainage that opens a break in the bluff line. Turn back to the left, now above the bluff line, passing interesting boulder formations atop which you can gain obscured views of the Nolin River Valley and beyond. Keep an eye open for house-size boulders below the trail.

Stay on the nose of a ridgeline and keep ascending to reach Houchins Ferry Road and the Temple Hill Trailhead at 6.4 miles. From here, the McCoy Hollow Trail starts across the gravel road toward the middle of the trailhead parking area. It leaves Temple Hill, travels 0.8 mile to Three Springs backcountry campsite, and continues for 4.9 more miles to intersect the Wet Prong–McCoy Hollow Connector Trail.

Good Spring Loop Trail

TYPE: Foot and horse

DIFFICULTY: Moderate

LENGTH: 7.6-mile loop

USE: Heavy

CONDITION: Mostly good

HIGHLIGHTS: Good Spring Church, homesites, Homestead backcountry campsite, Bluffs backcountry campsite, Collie Ridge backcountry campsite, good loop opportunity

CONNECTIONS: Turnhole Bend Trail, Buffalo Trail, Sal Hollow Trail, McCoy Hollow Trail, Collie Ridge Trail, Raymer Hollow Trail

ACCESS: To find Good Spring Loop Trail from the visitor center, take Mammoth Cave Parkway for 0.6 mile, then turn right onto Green River Ferry Road and continue for 3.4 miles to Maple Springs Road.

Wolf Trees

The forest in and around Mammoth Cave National Park features many of what foresters call wolf trees. These trees, obviously much larger than those of the surrounding forest, were once "lone wolves"—a white oak that once shaded a home, for example, or a tree in a grazing pasture. These trees typically have thick trunks and horizontal or outward-protruding branches. Since the park's inception, a forest has grown around these wolf trees. They are no longer alone, but they do stand out.

Wolf trees often serve to indicate old homesites.

Turn left and drive 1 mile to the Maple Springs Trailhead. Continue forward a short distance beyond Maple Springs Trailhead, turning left onto the gravel road leading to Good Spring Church. Follow this gravel road for 0.5 mile to reach the church and the trailhead. The direction of travel described above leaves left as you face the church.

The Good Spring Loop Trail makes a circuit through the heart of the park backcountry. Nearly every backcountry trail either connects to this path or comes close to it. This path starts at Good Spring Church and circles the valley of Dry Prong. It leaves westbound from the church, passing some springs that give the area its name, tracing old roads, first meeting the Turnhole Bend Trail, then the Buffalo Trail, and coming just yards from the Sal Hollow Trail. From there, it descends to the confluence of Dry Prong and Wet Prong Buffalo Creek, then traverses a rich bottomland before climbing back into the ridgetops where pioneer farms once stood. Passing the McCoy Hollow Trail, it joins Collie Ridge and runs north—in conjunction with the Collie Ridge Trail—before diverging back east, once again crossing the Dry Prong before climbing along a beech-dominant spring hollow and completing its loop. The loop is popular with equestrians and hikers alike, and backpackers should take note that three fine campsites are stretched along the way, making overnight treks on this trail a treat.

The loop is described traveling counterclockwise, which is the predominant direction of travel. Leave the Good Spring Church Trailhead and descend, with the church graveyard off to your right. Soon you'll step over the first of a few perennial springs while traveling under full-fledged woods. Note the ferns, beeches, and sycamores in the moist ravines. The stream flows expose flat limestone as they work downhill. The path braids in muddy areas, as horses and hikers avoid the mire.

At 0.6 mile the Turnhole Bend Trail leaves left and continues for 2.5 miles to the Turnhole Bend campsite, while intersecting the Buffalo and Sal Hollow Trails along the way. Just ahead, you'll pass the spur trail to Homestead campsite on your right. The Good Spring Loop Trail bridges another perennial spring branch, which emerges from the limestone wall visible from the bridge. The Good Spring Loop Trail continues westerly along the south rim of Dry Prong, which is well below you. Watch for a covered well in a cedar copse to the left of the trail. This well is an absolute indicator of a homestead. Occasionally the trail passes close enough to the rim to allow good views into the hollow below.

Begin circling a major but intermittent feeder branch of Dry Prong. Reach a high point and horse-tie area before descending to meet the Buffalo Trail at 2.4 miles. Here, the Buffalo Trail leads left for a few yards, turns left again to

Days of Old

Farmers in what is now Mammoth Cave National Park primarily grew tobacco and corn. In the days before cars or decent roads, they used the Green River to take their crops to market. They built flatboats, loaded them, and poled them down the Green to the Ohio, thence to the Mississippi and down to New Orleans, where they sold their crops and also the wood from the flatboats for the New Orleans housing market. They would then make the arduous and often dangerous journey back to Kentucky along the Natchez Trace, which traveled from Natchez, Mississippi, to Nashville. From Nashville they took the Cumberland Trace into the bluegrass country. Men often banded together during this late-fall trek, where robbery was often a possibility—not to mention cold temperatures and swollen streams. These travails inspired the farmers to concentrate their product, turning corn into "corn juice" or "squeezin's," also known as moonshine. This liquid corn was a lot easier to transport and had more value per pound, so the choice was a matter of simple economics.

meet the Sal Hollow Trail, then continues on for 2.8 miles to reach the Maple Springs Trailhead. The Good Spring Loop, however, veers right and continues as a wide track lined with tall trees, working downhill. At 2.7 miles, a spur trail leaves left to Bluffs backcountry campsite—one of the best and most popular camps in the park. A homesite, as indicated by yucca plants, lies on your right just past this junction. Work downhill along the nose of a ridge before making a sharp drop to saddle alongside an impressive bluff line. Here an undercut wall of rock offers a refuge from storms and also an aboveground connection to the underworld for which this park is more famously known. Resume the downgrade beyond the bluff. Notice the parallel eroded paths that were created long before this was a park.

At 3.3 miles, reach the flat hollow of lower Dry Prong at its confluence with Wet Prong. This gorgeous flat is one of my favorite areas in the park. It is rich with wildflowers in spring, tall with growth in summer, and colorful in fall. In winter you may find water here rushing toward the Green River, but most likely you will be stepping on the tan sandy streambed of Dry Prong rather than wading. As you cross, travel a short distance down the streambed to the actual confluence of the two prongs. I have had to wade at this point. Once the Green River was so high, it backed water into both prongs of Buffalo Creek.

Leave the stream and traverse a flat that can be muddy. This is the low point of the entire loop. Tall sycamores and other trees shade the flat. Watch for a

The Good Spring Church Cemetery inters former residents of what is now Mammoth Cave National Park.

twin-trunked sycamore just as you make your way uphill and out of the flat on a braided rock track. Level off in an oak-dominated ridgeline. Parts of this path can be quite brushy in summer. At 4.1 miles, reach a major four-way trail junction. To your left a spur trail leads to Collie Ridge backcountry campsite, which has a spring that emerges from the hillside and immediately forms a waterfall. Dead ahead, the McCoy Hollow Trail leads 5.7 miles to the Temple Hill Trailhead and also meets the Wet Prong–McCoy Hollow Connector Trail. To your right the Good Spring Loop Trail runs in conjunction with the Collie Ridge Trail, and now heads northeast along Collie Ridge. Here Collie Ridge divides Wet Prong and Dry Prong.

The Good Spring Loop Trail travels a wide and heavily traveled track, one very popular with horses; it can be dusty or muddy, depending on recent rains. Sand also gathers in spots. The ridge slopes away on both sides. Watch for wolf trees and old homesites along here. Old roadbeds spur off the track, which is shaded by large trees. Occasional rock slabs spill over the ridgetop. It's a nice, easy ramble on top of Collie Ridge—and before you know it the path has reached another trail junction at 5.3 miles. Here the Collie Ridge Trail continues forward for 2.4 miles to the Lincoln Trailhead on Ollie Road. The Good Spring Loop diverges acutely right, onto a narrower roadbed, now heading southbound. The shady track is mostly level.

Watch for a partially fallen sandstone block chimney to the right of the trail at 6.5 miles. A further look around this former homestead reveals seemingly haphazard piles of rock. These rocks were accumulated as the long-ago farmer cleared the soil for easier tilling. The Good Spring Loop Trail continues beyond the old chimney and drops into the hollow of Dry Prong, passing a streamlet. The bottomland here is much smaller than downstream. Notice how the streambed is also much rockier than below. Curve onto a hillside before entering a second hollow. To the left of the trail are metal relics from the past. The folks who abandoned them called these relics trash, but now they are historic artifacts from a lifeway fallen prey to modern times.

Reach a trail junction just ahead, at 7.2 miles. Here a spur trail leads forward and uphill a short distance to Raymer Hollow Trail. The Good Spring Loop Trail turns right here, bridging a perennial stream to enter a north-facing hollow that has a year-round creek of its own. This is one of the coolest, moistest places in the park—and it shows. Notice all the smooth, gray-trunked beech trees here. Beeches are draped in golden leaves during fall. Curiously, the leaves of younger beeches stay on through the winter, though they are dried and brown. This makes the tree easy for people to identify. Beech trees range throughout the United States east of the Mississippi River. Animals of cave country such as deer and turkey know this tree well, for it provides them the beechnut, an important food in their diet.

Ascend along this rich forest. You are back in the Good Spring area, and the branches you just crossed are part of those good springs. Level out near the Good Spring Church Cemetery before completing your loop at Good Spring Church at 7.6 miles.

TYPE: Foot and horse

DIFFICULTY: Difficult

LENGTH: 5.7 miles one-way

USE: Moderate

CONDITION: Mostly good

HIGHLIGHTS: Green River bluffs, views, boulder fields, Three Springs backcountry campsite, McCoy Hollow backcountry campsite

CONNECTIONS: First Creek Trail, Wet Prong–McCoy Hollow Connector Trail

ACCESS: To find McCoy Hollow Trail from the visitor center, take Mammoth Cave Parkway south for 2.9 miles to a split in the road. Veer right onto Highway 70, Brownsville Road. Follow Brownsville Road for 9.7 miles to an intersection. Turn right here and stay with Highway 70 for 0.3 mile to reach Houchins Ferry Road. Turn right onto Houchins Ferry Road and follow it for 1.8 miles to the ferry. From the ferry, take Houchins Ferry Road 1.9 miles to the Temple Hill Trailhead.

McCoy Hollow Trail runs along, around, and above the bluffs of the Green River, in the western edge of the park's backcountry area. The path winds in and out of hollows that are open by the river and tighten up the farther they are from the water. Level midvalley areas, known as benches, are often where the trail goes when it works around these valleys that flow into the Green River. The feeder branches have bluffs and rock features of their own, including cascades cut by water, just as the inner underground passages of Mammoth Cave were also cut by water. Trail treaders pay a price for all the scenery they see. Despite the level benches upon which the path passes, it also has many ups and downs, so expect a challenge on this track.

The McCoy Hollow Trail leaves Temple Hill Trailhead, descending easterly in hickory-oak woodlands onto an increasingly sloped hillside. The path turns into a steep hollow, cutting a watery path to the Green River. It then reaches a level area and makes a sharp left, heading east. The Green River comes into view on your right. An impressive bluff, with overhanging rocks, borders the trail to your left. This and other bluffs are reminiscent of the bluffs and rock shelters of eastern Kentucky. Curve away from the Green River and into a feeder branch hollow to intersect the spur trail to Three Springs backcountry campsite at 0.8 mile. The Three Springs camp is set in a nice flat alongside the feeder branch 0.1 mile from the McCoy Hollow Trail.

The McCoy Hollow Trail straddles a wildflower-covered flat between the Green River and this overhanging bluff.

The McCoy Hollow Trail continues upstream along the feeder branch, curving around the springs that gave the Three Spring campsite its name. After the spring crossings the path follows the hollow downstream as the creek drops off below. The path curves into another hollow, passing a waterfall at 1.5 miles that is audible but not visible from the trail. The recovery pool is surprisingly deep for such a small stream. McCoy Hollow Trail then repeats its pattern, curving around the head of this hollow and returning downstream. The path passes the waterfall a second time, then abruptly turns left, climbing steeply atop a rocky grade, leaving the lush hollow for dry hickory-oak woods. Cross the uppermost reaches of a streambed before topping out on a ridgeline at 2 miles. Notice the old roadbed traveling along the ridgeline.

From this high point the path drops, finding a break in a bluff line to reach a perennial stream at 2.3 miles. Cross this stream at a pretty bluff line and join a level bench. The bluffs continue to your left, and the stream makes its way down to the Green River. The level bench makes for easy travel. The hollow widens. The Green River is dead ahead; the path, however, makes a sharp left at a rock pile, left over from field clearing. It ascends the nose of a rocky ridge, beginning an extended climb, using switchbacks to moderate the grade. The path is now well above the Green River, and reaches an upper cliff line. Boulders have fallen from this cliff line and add to the woodland scenery as the McCoy Hollow Trail winds among the gray backs that are cloaked with moss on their shady sides.

After meandering amid the boulders, the path turns abruptly left and makes the top of the ridge, cutting through a break in the cliff line. It resumes its northeasterly direction before reaching at trail junction at 3.6 miles. Here a spur trail leads 0.1 mile to the McCoy Hollow backcountry campsite. This campsite stands on the edge of a drop extending all the way to the Green River, not visible through the trees. Cedars and oaks shade the site. Water is a problem here, and must be accessed from streams either 1.3 miles back or 0.8 mile ahead on the McCoy Hollow Trail.

The path leaves the junction and passes three sinkholes, then works its way down, passing a couple of streams at 4.4 miles. From here, the trail climbs again to curve around the point of a ridge and come along a bluff line to your left. Note the reddish coloration on this bluff line, from iron oxidization. A big switchback to the right cuts through a break in the rocks. Ahead, as the trail descends, an old chimney stands off to the right, through the woods. In summer the chimney may be obscured by trees. Descend farther through a boulder field and come to Wet Prong at 5.1 miles. This perennial stream can be easily rock-hopped in times of normal flow. Turn upstream in lush bottomland before leaving the creek and ascending. Intersect the McCoy Hollow–Wet Prong Connector at 5.3 miles. Here the connector trail leads left 0.5 mile to the Wet Prong Loop Trail.

The McCoy Hollow Trail climbs away from the junction to reach a bench and curves into a tributary of Wet Prong, crossing its uppermost reaches. Keep ascending to meet the Collie Ridge Trail at 5.7 miles. A spur trail leads acutely right 0.2 mile to the Collie Ridge backcountry campsite. One portion of the Good Spring Loop Trail leads right; it's 0.8 mile down to Dry Prong, 1.4 miles to Bluffs backcountry campsite, and 1.7 miles to intersect the Buffalo Trail. To your left the Collie Ridge Trail leads left 3.6 miles to the Lincoln Trailhead. Also to your left the Good Spring Loop Trail runs in conjunction with the Collie Ridge Trail for 1.2 miles, then leaves right 2.3 more miles back to Good Spring Church.

Raymer Hollow Trail

TYPE: Foot and horse

DIFFICULTY: Moderate to difficult

LENGTH: 5.3 miles one-way

USE: Moderate

CONDITION: Mostly good

HIGHLIGHTS: Waterfalls, settler cemetery, Raymer Hollow backcountry campsite

CONNECTIONS: Good Spring Loop Trail, Collie Ridge Trail, Blair Spring Trail

ACCESS: To find Raymer Hollow Trail from the visitor center, take Mammoth Cave Parkway 0.6 mile; turn right onto Green River Ferry Road and drive 3.4 miles to Maple Springs Road. Turn left and follow Maple Springs Road 1 mile to the Maple Springs Trailhead. This trail starts on Maple Springs Road 0.6 mile north of the trailhead.

The Raymer Hollow Trail starts all by itself on the north side of Maple Springs Loop Road. It then winds its way along the upper watershed of Dry Prong Buffalo Creek. Raymer Hollow backcountry campsite is located along the trail at 4.3 miles. The path leaves Maple Springs Road 0.6 mile north of the Maple Springs Trailhead, the primary jumping-off point for backcountry users. Pass around a pole gate and follow an old roadbed in an upland hardwood forest dotted with cedar. The wide track tops a hill then dips to cross a small stream. A homesite sits immediately to the right of the trail beyond the creek.

The hollow to your left drops off steeply. As you walk the old road, note the larger trees along its margin. They may have shaded a wagon or two in days gone by. At 0.6 mile the old roadbed drops left toward Dry Prong Buffalo

A backcountry waterfall along the Raymer Hollow Trail noisily descends, ultimately to flow underground and shape Mammoth Cave.

Creek and meets a spur trail connecting to Good Spring Loop Trail. The Raymer Hollow Trail leaves right, narrows, and begins to resemble a woodland path. White oaks and other dry-situation upland hardwoods shade the trail until it curves widely to the north. Beech trees then become more common. Dry Prong is well below to your left. Ascend to circle a drainage. If you listen closely, you'll hear a hillside spring dropping over rock to form a little but noisy waterfall. Ahead, piles of rock indicate former cleared land. The rocks were gathered and piled up to make the soil more tillable. Just ahead, at 1.6 miles, a large rocky sinkhole lies to the left of the trail. The top layer of sandstone has collapsed due to limestone erosion below the sandstone.

Stay along the edge of the valley. Obscured views of Collie Ridge open to the west. In the forest around you, the widespread crowns of old trees tower over a younger forest. Much of Mammoth Cave National Park was cultivated as small farms; thus much of the forest here is relatively young. Look for more rock piles along the path. Dip to a small branch and turn away from the valley edge, now heading easterly in gently rolling land. Cross other streamlets and begin to curve back to the northwest. Gain a ridgeline to reach a cemetery on your left at 3.7 miles. Simple unmarked stones mark the interred, who once called what is now the national park home. The graveyard, one of seventy within the park bounds, was landscaped with periwinkle, which has now spread throughout the immediate area. A large sinkhole lies to the right of the trail near the cemetery.

Rejoin the edge of Dry Prong Valley beyond the cemetery and then descend steeply to the creek. Just before you reach Dry Prong, a trail leaves left from a huge beech tree to reach a falls. This cascade drops about 12 feet over a rock bluff. The moist site is home to myriad wildflowers in spring. The Raymer Hollow Trail reaches Dry Prong just beyond the beech tree, at 4.1 miles. "Dry" Prong, usually flowing at this point, is easily crossed on rocks. The path follows this prong downstream in bottomland then ascends steeply to reach the spur trail to Raymer Hollow campsite at 4.3 miles. This spur path extends 0.3 mile to the camp, which is located just above Dry Prong. Rock bluffs adorn the stream near the campsite and make for interesting exploration.

A homesite is located at the junction of Raymer Hollow Trail and the campsite spur trail. Metal relics add life to the site. Look but leave them for others to discover and enjoy. Curve around the homesite and stay along above the rim of a feeder branch, heading northwest. The level trail undulates to traverse a couple of small branches. The path steepens as it aims for Collie Ridge; you'll reach the ridgetop at 5.3 miles. A hitching post is located here at the trail junction. To your right the Collie Ridge Trail leads 1.9 miles to the Lincoln Trailhead. To your left, it meets the Good Spring Loop Trail in 0.5 mile. The Blair Spring Trail continues forward 1.2 miles to meet the Wet Prong of Buffalo Loop Trail.

TYPE: Foot and bicycle

DIFFICULTY: Moderate to difficult

LENGTH: 8.1 miles one-way

USE: Moderate to heavy

CONDITION: Good

HIGHLIGHTS: Springs, wildflowers, Sal Hollow backcountry campsite

CONNECTIONS: Good Spring Loop Trail, Buffalo Trail, Turnhole Bend Trail

ACCESS: To find Sal Hollow Trail from the visitor center, take Mammoth Cave Parkway 0.6 mile. Turn right onto Green River Ferry Road and follow it for 3.4 miles to Maple Springs Loop Road. Turn left and continue 1 mile to the Maple Springs Trailhead. The Sal Hollow Trail starts on the west side of Maple Springs Loop Road.

This trail is unique in that it's open to mountain bikes and closed to horses. The result is a less muddy surface, especially on hills. Mountain bikers take advantage of this, the only backcountry trail open to them; it's also an important trail for those wanting to make a loop of the entire Mammoth Cave backcountry. Sal Hollow Trail begins at the Maple Springs Trailhead and works its way west along the upper bluffs of the Green River, traveling through a heavily settled area before leaving an old road then winding past a bluff opening, from which emanates a spring. Beyond this the trail curves along the contour of the Green River before crossing the Turnhole Bend Trail. It keeps along the rim of the Green River before dropping into Sal Hollow, then climbs to the hilltops, passing the Sal Hollow backcountry campsite before turning away from the Green River and meeting the Buffalo Trail.

The Sal Hollow Trail heads southwest from the Maple Springs Trailhead on a gravel track overlaid on grass. Soon you'll enter young forestland and begin to follow an old roadbed bordered in pines, cedars, and hardwoods. The trail keeps a southwesterly direction, passing through a once heavily settled area. At 0.5 mile the roadbed reaches a wooden fence, blocking further passage. Here the Sal Hollow Trail leaves the old roadbed and bears right, now on a small path.

The trail wanders around rib ridges and into mostly dry hollows before descending to an unmistakable feature at 1.3 miles: the first of two bluff springs. To your right, a steep rock bluff is punctured by emerging water at its base. A short trail leads to the base of the bluff. This spring demonstrates part of the complicated relationship between rock and water here at Mammoth Cave. Throughout this park, water flows into, through, and out of the cave complex.

The Pawpaw

Pawpaw bushes reproduce via root sprouts, which means they're often found together in groups. They have large leaves, 6 to 12 inches in length, which droop like their tropical cousins farther south. Their yellow banana-like fruit are favored by wildlife, especially raccoons and 'possums. Settlers made bread and puddings from pawpaw fruits. Attempts have been made to cultivate pawpaw as a fruit tree; Kentucky is near the center of its range.

Ascend from the bluff spring, passing a homesite to the right of the trail before topping out. The land drops off sharply to your left and is level to your right. At 1.8 miles, pass a conspicuous rocky sink about 20 feet to the left of the trail. It is deep and bordered with mossy rock below the surface and looks almost like an overgrown well. Ahead, pick up an old roadbed and cross a rocky streambed emerging from a cedar copse on your right. The trail cruises the edge of the wooded rim descending to the Green River. In other places the trail dips into shallow coves before returning to the rim. Pawpaw bushes form an understory here.

The Sal Hollow Trail now crosses a draw and ascends to a cedar copse, meeting the Turnhole Bend Trail at 3.5 miles. From here it's 1.1 mile left to the end of the Turnhole Bend Trail, and 0.7 mile right to the Buffalo Trail. The Sal Hollow Trail leaves the Turnhole Bend Trail, dipping into shallow drainages leading left toward the Green River. At 4.1 miles you'll pass a sink to the right of the trail that sometimes holds water. More sinks lie ahead after the trail passes through a boulder field.

The Sal Hollow Trail then crosses some particularly evident old roads. The track is level as you pass a sinkhole on your left. Descend a dry streambed then pass a homesite marked by a semiclear area with a massive white oak shading the locale. Descend more to reach a second cave spring at 5.4 miles. This one also emerges from a bluff hillside. More old roads lace the area beyond the spring. The rocky trail switchbacks downhill, passing a huge white oak on one of the switchbacks to enter cedar woods. Off to your right at 6 miles, among the cedars, is a block chimney from an old homesite. Look around also for metal relics from the days when a farmer and his family lived here. More than 580 farms were bought out by the state of Kentucky during land acquisition for the park. Land generally fetched $30 per acre. Many residents didn't want to sell but were forced out through the use of eminent domain.

The trail turns up Sal Hollow before descending to cross the stream that formed the hollow at 6.2 miles. The stream often runs dry below this crossing. If you are staying at Sal Hollow backcountry campsite, look for water here. If

Bluebells often form carpets in flats along park streams.

there isn't any, follow the streambed down to the Green River. The path crosses the bottomland of Sal Hollow, filled with bluebells in spring, then curves left. It formerly turned directly up a rocky ridgeline but has been rerouted at a more manageable grade. The streambed is below you as the path angles uphill, and then makes a hard switchback to the right, still climbing, to reach a trail junction at 7 miles. Here a spur trail leads acutely left to reach Sal Hollow backcountry campsite. Keep an eye open for above-normal-size oaks and beech trees in the forest.

The path meanders past a dry streambed along the level bench, with hill and rock to your left and land falling away to your right. It then leaves the bench and curves right in classic upland hardwoods around a side hollow that falls into Sal Hollow. Briefly follow an old road and veer left, uphill. The Sal Hollow Trail crosses a streambed by wooden bridge then keeps ascending through tall woods. It ends after intersecting the Buffalo Trail at 8.1 miles. To your right, the Buffalo Trail leads 1.7 miles to the Turnhole Bend Trail and 1.1 more miles back to Maple Springs Trailhead. To your left it travels a few feet down a road, then leaves right to meet the Good Spring Loop Trail just a few feet farther along.

Turnhole Bend Trail

TYPE: Foot and horse

DIFFICULTY: Easy to moderate

LENGTH: 2.5 miles one-way

USE: Moderate to heavy

CONDITION: Mostly good

HIGHLIGHTS: Old homesites, good connector trail, Turnhole Bend backcountry campsite

CONNECTIONS: Good Spring Loop Trail, Buffalo Trail, Sal Hollow Trail

ACCESS: The Turnhole Bend Trail is an internal trail. It can be accessed on its north end by walking for 0.6 mile on the Good Spring Loop Trail from Good Spring Church Trailhead, or near its south end by taking the Sal Hollow Trail for 3.5 miles from the Maple Springs Trailhead.

This north–south path runs from the Good Spring Loop Trail southward, roughly tracing an old road to meet the Buffalo Trail. From there it follows a regraded old roadbed, making for easy walking. Big trees preside over younger woods, marking places where settlers either lived or left shade trees. Beyond the Sal Hollow Trail junction, the path traverses a narrow ridge with the Green River snaking around it on both sides, the Turnhole Bend. The official trail ends at the Turnhole Bend backcountry campsite, but the old trail that once continued to the Green River can still be followed.

The Turnhole Bend Trail leaves south from the Good Spring Loop Trail at a homesite. Follow a narrow trail that parallels an old road. The path rolls through tall trees past a second homesite to the left of the trail. It then crosses a small streambed in a shallow cove before intersecting the Buffalo Trail at 0.7 mile. Here the Buffalo Trail leads left for 1.1 miles back to Good Spring Church Trailhead, and right for 1.7 miles to intersect the Sal Hollow Trail. The Turnhole Bend Trail now follows a wider roadbed, keeping south and climbing. Tall roadside and forest trees are leftovers from the settlement era. White oak trees with widespread crowns are the most noticeable of these leftovers. Top out then make a downgrade to reach the Sal Hollow Trail at 1.4 miles. From here the Sal Hollow Trail leads left 3.5 miles back to Maple Springs Trailhead, and right 4.6 miles to meet the Buffalo Trail.

The Turnhole Bend Trail leaves south from the Sal Hollow Trail, still on a wide roadbed. The path descends slightly in a young forest. At 1.7 miles, pass a homesite on your right. Continue the downgrade as the ridgeline you are on continues to narrow. The Green River is on both sides of the ridge. The ridge begins to widen before reaching a large sinkhole to the left of the trail and the intersection with the spur trail to Turnhole Bend backcountry campsite at 2.5 miles. This spur trail leaves left on a spindly land bridge above a sink to reach a knob and level camp at 0.1 mile.

Wet Prong of Buffalo Loop Trail

TYPE: Half foot and horse, half foot only

DIFFICULTY: Easy to moderate

LENGTH: 5.2-mile loop

USE: Moderate to heavy

CONDITION: Mostly good

HIGHLIGHTS: Streamside trail, bluffs, good loop trail, Ferguson Hollow backcountry campsite

CONNECTIONS: First Creek Trail, Wet Prong–McCoy Hollow Connector Trail, Blair Spring Trail

ACCESS: To find Wet Prong of Buffalo Loop Trail from the visitor center, head south on Mammoth Cave Parkway 0.6 mile. Turn right onto Green River Ferry Road and follow it for 1.3 miles, then continue for 5.7 miles to Highway 1827. Turn left onto Highway 1827 and follow it for 1.1 miles. Turn left onto Ollie Road and follow it for 2.7 miles to Houch-ins Ferry Road. Make another left turn here, following Houchins Ferry Road for 0.1 mile to reach the First Creek Trailhead on your right.

This trail forms a loop, leaving from the First Creek Trailhead and descending into the Wet Prong Buffalo Creek Valley before turning up the main stream and crossing Wet Prong Buffalo Creek several times. This valley is quite beautiful, as it features a bluff-bordered branch of the Green River that flows year-round amid a lush forest of beech and magnolia trees, among other flora. The creek crossings can be made dry-footed most of the year, exceptions being early spring and after heavy rains.

Fall leaves land on a sandbar of Wet Prong Buffalo Creek.

The trail leaves First Creek Trailhead, located in the park's north end, and crosses Houchins Ferry Road, heading southeast. You'll immediately enter pine-dominated woodland. This forest is in transition. Once fields, the area grew up with pines, pioneering the forest. In their shade grow the future kings of the area, the maples, oaks, and hickories. You can see many fallen pines now. More will fall over time; in a generation or two, nary a pine will be found. The path undulates through this transitional forest to reach at trail junction at 0.6 mile. A pair of horse-hitching posts are located in the level area. Here begins the loop portion of the Wet Prong Buffalo Loop. Keep right; the trail leaving left is your return route.

The Wet Prong of Buffalo Loop Trail keeps on a ridgeline that helps keep your feet dry longer, as the upper end of the loop crosses the Wet Prong, thereby raising the possibility of wet feet. Equestrians needn't worry about wet feet for two reasons: First, of course, they won't be walking; second, the upper portion of the trail—the part with more fords—is closed to horses. White oaks dominate the ridge, which forms a divide between branches of Wet Prong.

A mild but steady downgrade leads toward Wet Prong. Tan sands and clay form the trailbed as the path finally reaches a feeder branch of Wet Prong. Despite the sometimes dry nature of the stream, this is a moist hollow, as evidenced by the presence of beech and magnolia trees. Step over the streambed three times in short order; by now, the stream normally flows full time. Look for a small waterfall on your left, just beyond the third crossing. This fall drops over a rock ledge. Rock bluffs also begin to appear along the stream.

From this point, the stream dives toward Wet Prong, while the trail makes a more gradual descent, gently curving into the Wet Prong Valley. Make a short but sharp drop to reach the flowing waters of Wet Prong Buffalo Creek at 2.1 miles. The name *Wet Prong* evolved in contrast to the Dry Prong of Buffalo Creek. Wet Prong is a perennial stream, flowing year-round, while Dry Prong flows only during winter, spring, and after heavy rains. It is the flowing nature of Wet Prong that makes it such an attractive stream, a place where you can enjoy the ever-moving, ever-changing temperament of water.

The trail makes the first of many fords of Wet Prong. Save for spring and following heavy rains, these can be rock-hopped by hikers with a lot of balance and a little nerve. Here the Wet Prong intersects the Wet Prong–McCoy Hollow Connector Trail, which leaves right 0.5 mile to meet the McCoy Hollow Trail.

From this point upstream, Wet Prong of Buffalo Loop Trail is open only to hikers. You will see that this regulation is blatantly disregarded. The trail turns up the creek, where small sand- and gravel bars form a narrow line between stream and woodland, where the clear waters flow over rocks and fallen trees, gurgling toward the Green River, where clear pools harbor darting minnows and other aquatic life. The trail winds its way up the thickly forested valley that is sometimes bordered by moss-, vine-, and fern-covered bluffs that peer down into Wet Prong. Gorgeous streamside flats covered in mountain laurel contrast with the valley walls rising upward.

At 3.3 miles, look on trail right for a particularly interesting bluff across the creek. The lower part of the bluff hanging over the water has fallen, and the flat slate-like pieces of fallen rock, lying on the edge of the creek, resemble a laid-out deck of cards. The upper part of the bluff still hangs high, but will one day fall and become erosion fodder for Wet Prong.

Make the final crossing at 3.8 miles. Two branches, nearly equal in size, come together at this point. The trail continues up the right branch just a short distance to reach a trail junction. The Blair Spring Trail has come 1.2 miles from Collie Ridge Trail. The Wet Prong of Buffalo Loop turns left here, and begins its way up the left branch into Wildcat Hollow, which flows perennially. The elevation gain increases as it meets the spur trail to the Ferguson backcountry campsite at 4.1 miles. Keep in an ever-narrowing hollow to span the branch on a wooden bridge. Just ahead, after one more bridge, is Blue Spring, the reason this stream is perennial. Blue Spring emerges clear, with a bluish cast, from the base of a hill in a rock vent. Upstream from here, the streambed will likely be dry. Dry or not, the Wet Prong of Buffalo Loop Trail curves left and leaves the valley, climbing into hickory-oak woods to reach the end of the loop portion of the trail at 4.6 miles. It is 0.6 mile from this junction back to the First Creek Trailhead.

Wet Prong–McCoy Hollow Connector Trail

TYPE: Foot and horse

DIFFICULTY: Easy to moderate

LENGTH: 0.5 mile one-way

USE: Moderate to heavy

CONDITION: Fair to good

HIGHLIGHTS: Connects Wet Prong Buffalo Trail and McCoy Hollow Trail

CONNECTIONS: Wet Prong of Buffalo Loop Trail, McCoy Hollow Trail

ACCESS: The Wet Prong–McCoy Hollow Connector Trail is an internal trail. Its north end can be reached via the Wet Prong of Buffalo Loop Trail. The south end can be reached via the McCoy Hollow Trail.

This is the shortest backcountry trail in the park. It serves to connect the Wet Prong of Buffalo Loop Trail and the McCoy Hollow Trail. The path leaves the Wet Prong of Buffalo Loop Trail beside the flowing waters of Wet Prong and climbs to a more level area on the side of the valley. At this point the path turns downstream well above Wet Prong, shaded by a rich deciduous forest dominated by oaks. The path curves with the valley and passes over a pair of streamlets. To your left the valley rises; to your right it drops off to Wet Prong. The level part of the valley narrows before intersecting the McCoy Hollow Trail at 0.5 mile. From this junction it is 0.5 mile left to the Collie Ridge Trail, and to your right, it reaches Houchins Ferry Road at 5.3 miles.

A sandstone chimney along the White Oak Trail stands in mute testimony to the residents that once dwelled in this park.

White Oak Trail

TYPE: Foot and horse

DIFFICULTY: Moderate

LENGTH: 5.0 miles out-and-back

USE: Low

CONDITION: Very good

HIGHLIGHTS: Homesites, rock overhang, riverside campsite

CONNECTIONS: None

ACCESS: To find the White Oak Trail from the visitor center, take Mammoth Cave Parkway for 0.6 mile. Turn right onto Green River Ferry Road and follow it for 1.3 miles to Green River Ferry. Cross Green River Ferry, staying with Green River Ferry Road for 4.5 more miles to reach Little Jordan Road, which is also known as Ugly Creek Road. Turn right and follow Little Jordan Road for 4.3 miles to reach the trailhead on your right.

The White Oak Trail is not connected to any other backcountry trail. Located in the northeastern corner of the park, it follows old roads from Little Jordan Road/Ugly Creek Road south to the Green River and what once was Dennison Ferry. The actual ferry has been long abandoned, but the trail ends just across the river from the Dennison Ferry Picnic Area. One of the park's best backcountry campsites, White Oak, is located at the trail's end.

Leave the small gravel parking area and pass around a pole gate, passing an information signboard. The wide track travels beneath hickory, oak, and pine. Like most other park trails, it is overlaid upon an old roadbed. Taller older trees border the path. True to its name, many white oaks populate the woods.

At 0.8 mile, dip into a flat, crossing a dry branch. Along the way the path turns at angles, reflecting old property lines, heading south and east. At 1.7 miles, on your right, is a limestone block chimney typical of cave country settlers. This chimney is nearly intact. You can see the outline of the old house, though cedars have reclaimed the area.

The White Oak Trail descends beyond the chimney. At this point, especially in winter, you can glimpse the Green River. Turn east along a steep slope, then reach a bluff's edge overlooking the Green. Here more views can be had of the watercourse that cut the valley causing Mammoth Cave. Wind ever downward, turning away from the bluff to enter piney woods. The forest soon reverts to lush hardwoods as you near the Green. At 2.5 miles the trail ends at the White Oak backcountry campsite. Sycamores, beeches, and maples shade the attractive site, which has a fine river view. Do not pass up the chance to get closer to the river and view a 300-plus-year-old sycamore with a huge trunk. Direct river access is tough, though, due to steep mud banks. Also, be aware that noise from the Dennison Ferry Picnic Area is clearly audible from this camp.

Exploring Aboveground: The Rails and Roads

The roads of Mammoth Cave offer some fine opportunities for exploring, whether by mountain bike, road bike, or scenic car tour. Luckily, the park visitor center is located in the heart of the park and makes for an ideal jumping off point to engage in all the above endeavors. Recent improvements to Mammoth Cave Parkway, Cave City Road, Maple Springs Road, and other park infrastructure make the journey better still. So read the following descriptions, then get out there and start touring!

Trail Biking

Pedaling opportunities have improved at the national park over the last few years. Expect them to get better. At one time, the Headquarters Bicycle Trail was the single venue for pedalers. Then Sal Hollow Trail was opened to mountain bikers (see "The Trails" chapter, page 72). As of late, the Mammoth Cave Railroad Bike and Hike Trail has given visitors an exciting new chance to get out and cycle. As of this writing, only a portion of the trail is open, but the plan is to extend the Bike and Hike Trail from Interstate 65 all the way to the park visitor center. Stay tuned as the path evolves.

Headquarters Campground Bike Trail

TYPE: Bicycle and foot

DIFFICULTY: Easy

LENGTH: 1 mile one-way

USE: Moderate to heavy

CONDITION: Excellent, gravel

HIGHLIGHTS: Elevated boardwalks

CONNECTIONS: None

ACCESS: This bike trail starts at Headquarters Campground.

Begin at Headquarters Campground. The trail leaves east on a paved path, shortly reaching Green River Ferry Road. From here the trail picks up an old train berm, the former Mammoth Cave Railroad, through the woods. This area is plentiful with deer, do not be surprised if you see some of these four-legged critters in this vicinity. Oaks, hickory, cedar, and dogwood border the trail. Mammoth Cave Parkway is off in the woods to your left. The trail then crosses two elevated boardwalks over wetlands before jogging left to reach the road heading to the Carmichael cave entrance. Bikers can turn left on the Carmichael Entrance road to reach Mammoth Cave Parkway and loop back to Headquarters Campground, or simply backtrack.

Mammoth Cave Railroad Bike and Hike Trail

TYPE: Bicycle and foot

DIFFICULTY: Moderate, with some very steep grades

CAUTION: *This is not a typical rail-trail. Watch for steep grades.*

LENGTH: 4.5 miles one-way

USE: Moderate

CONDITION: Excellent, gravel

HIGHLIGHTS: Mostly follows old railroad grade connecting Park City to Mammoth Cave National Park, historic sites

CONNECTIONS: None

ACCESS: The Mammoth Cave Railroad Bike and Hike Trail starts at Sloans Crossing Pond and ends at Zion Cemetery Road.

This bicycle trail is an ongoing addition to the park trail system and promises to be a huge hit with park visitors. When it is finished the path will generally

Relic cars from the old Mammoth Cave Railroad brought early tourists to visit the underground sights.

trace the former Mammoth Cave Railroad, which connected Mammoth Cave to the old Louisville & Nashville Railroad, which in turn passed through what was then known as Glasgow Junction and is now Park City. The trail will follow the old railroad berm as much as possible. Historical and natural wayside exhibits will enhance the experience. When the trail is completed, it will run from Mammoth Cave Hotel through Sloans Crossing Pond and to Zion Cemetery Road. Someday it may connect to Park City.

Currently the finished part of the trail begins at Sloans Crossing Pond and heads toward Zion Cemetery Road. Sloans Crossing has a picnic area and parking.

The Mammoth Cave Railroad Bike and Hike Trail parallels the Mammoth Cave Parkway until it crosses it again. You'll then pass the site of Proctor's Hotel, and another community known as Union City, amid wetlands. Reach Locust Grove Cemetery and a parking area before crossing Mammoth Cave

Parkway twice in succession, near the intersection of the parkway and Highways 255/70.

From this point, the bike-and-hike trail makes a southerly run along the strip of park land that Mammoth Cave Parkway follows. This segment is more hilly. Pass the Dripping Springs Escarpment before reaching Diamond Caverns, a private cave that has been in operation a long time. Parking is available at Diamond Caverns. The trail keeps toward Interstate 65 and crosses back over to the west side of the road just before Zion Cemetery Road. It currently ends at Zion Cemetery Road, which also has parking.

Road Biking

The roads of Mammoth Cave offer some fine bicycling. The roads are all two lanes, have reasonable speed limits for cars, and feature pavement in mostly good condition, especially the roads entirely within the park. The terrain here isn't too hilly, and the landscape is appealing. The following are suggested road biking rides, all of them running entirely on paved roads.

Doyel Valley Ride

ROADS USED: Mammoth Cave Parkway, Highways 255/70, Highway 255, Cave City Road

DIFFICULTY: Moderate

LENGTH: 12.5-mile loop

HIGHLIGHTS: Doyel Valley Overlook, Sloans Crossing Pond, Sand Cave

FACILITIES: Water, restrooms at visitor center

The Doyel Valley Ride forms a loop that is mostly inside the park. It makes the most of the nice paved road of Mammoth Cave Parkway heading out toward Park City. Pedalers can also incorporate the Mammoth Cave Railroad Bike and Hike Trail into part of this loop. Leave the visitor center and follow Mammoth Cave Parkway, passing Cave City Road—your return route. Keep on to the Doyel Valley Overlook at 2 miles. This is a good place to look out over the park terrain. From here, reach the intersection with Highway 70 after a bit of a climb. Veer left here, staying with Mammoth Cave Parkway. Sloans Crossing Pond, with a picnic area, is on your right. The road levels out and you reach an intersection at 5 miles. Keep forward here, temporarily leaving the park on Highways 255/70. The Mammoth Cave Railroad Bike and Hike Trail leaves to your right. Continue on Highways 255/70 until you reach a T-intersection at 6.7 miles and turn left, heading back toward the park on Cave City Road. Pass Sand

Cave on your right at the park entrance, then stay straight on a gently curving and mostly level roadway in great shape to reach Mammoth Cave Parkway once again at 11 miles. Turn right and backtrack 1.3 miles to the visitor center.

Houchins Valley Road Ride

ROADS USED: Mammoth Cave Parkway, Cave City Road, Park Ridge Road, Flint Ridge Road

DIFFICULTY: Moderate

LENGTH: 13-mile loop

HIGHLIGHTS: Sand Cave, Mammoth Cave Baptist Church

FACILITIES: Water, restrooms at visitor center

This is a good road ride for casual pedalers who want to experience Mammoth Cave without spending all day on a bike. The area around the visitor center may be a bit busy, but otherwise the roads used here are quieter than your average roads outside the park. Furthermore, park speed limits are lower than you'll find on other public roads.

Leave the visitor center on Mammoth Cave Parkway; follow the parkway for 1.3 miles to Cave City Road. Turn left onto Cave City Road on a pleasant winding two-lane track. At 4 miles Park Ridge Road leaves left. If you wish, you can go just a short bit on Cave City Road beyond Park Ridge Road to visit Sand Cave, via a short all-access trail. The road pedal follows Park Ridge Road, which travels through the park then along its border. The roadway has a few rough patches, but it's all paved as it passes farmland on your right and park woodlands on your left. At 9 miles, turn left onto Flint Ridge Road and fully reenter park lands. This road is winding and has more hills than the rest of the loop, especially toward the end. At 13 miles, return to the visitor center.

Ollie Ridge There-and-Back Ride

ROADS USED: Mammoth Cave Parkway, Green River Ferry Road, Maple Springs Loop Road, Highway 1352, Highway 1827, Ollie Road, Ollie Ridge Road

DIFFICULTY: Moderate

LENGTH: 32 miles out-and-back

HIGHLIGHTS: Green River Ferry, Maple Springs, quiet roads much of way

FACILITIES: Water, restrooms at visitor center, picnic area and restrooms at Maple Springs trailhead, country store

This ride explores the north side of the park and some state-maintained roads on the north end of the park. Leave the visitor center and turn right onto Green River Ferry Road, which makes a solid downgrade to the Green River Ferry. Take the ferry across the Green River then climb back out of the valley to reach Maple Springs Loop Road, which makes a pleasant circuit through attractive woodland. There is a picnic area at the actual Maple Springs Trailhead. Beyond the trailhead, Maple Springs Road becomes narrower and a little rougher—though it *is* paved—and has some vertical variation.

Ride on a quality surface after rejoining Green River Ferry Road, leaving the park and continuing forward on Highway 1352, a Kentucky Scenic Byway, to reach Highway 1827 at 9 miles. There's a country store at this intersection. Turn left onto Highway 1827 and follow it 1.2 miles to quiet Ollie Road. This quaint road exemplifies rural south-central Kentucky farm and ridge country. At 13 miles, veer right onto Ollie Ridge Road. At this point, gravel Houchins Ferry Road continues forward. Paved Ollie Ridge Road, a dead-end thoroughfare, offers more quiet and rustic pedaling. At 16 miles, reach the Great Onyx Job Corps Center, a job training facility for youth. After you pass under the sign indicating the center, turn around; the facility is monitored for visitors. From this point, backtrack 16 miles to the visitor center on the same route.

Scenic Driving

Scenic car touring offers an unparalleled chance to gain the big-picture, overall view of Mammoth Cave National Park on a single trip.

Mammoth Cave Park Scenic Loop Drive

TYPE: Paved and gravel

LENGTH: 60-mile loop

HIGHLIGHTS: Green River Ferry, Good Spring Church, Big Woods, Houchins Ferry, Turnhole Bend Nature Trail, Sloans Crossing Pond, Sand Cave, Dennison Ferry Picnic Area

AMENITIES: Stores, restaurants, picnic areas

ACCESS: This scenic drive starts at the visitor center.

This scenic drive takes in the whole of the park. The roads are mostly paved with some gravel tracks, but all roads can be handled by normal passenger vehicles. Do note, however, that Little Jordan Road/Ugly Creek Road can be a little bumpy and has a low-water bridge that makes for a dry and doable crossing 95 percent of the time.

Your adventure starts at the hub of all activity in Mammoth Cave, the visitor center. Backtrack on Mammoth Cave Parkway 0.6 mile to Green River Ferry Road. Turn right here and descend into the Green River Valley. The Green River Ferry area has short trails where you can explore the woods around you, especially the Echo River Springs, a short spring run that contains the outflow from the waters coursing through the actual Mammoth Cave.

You'll now experience your first of two auto ferry rides across the Green River. These ferries are relics of days gone by, before bridges were as common as they are today. The park-run ferry leads across the Green River into the less visited north side of the park. Densely wooded Green River Ferry Road climbs from the river to reach Maple Springs Loop Road. Turn left onto Maple Springs Loop Road, passing the Maple Springs Trailhead, which has a picnic area and restrooms as well as access to Sal Hollow and other trails.

Just beyond the Maple Springs Trailhead, the tour turns left onto Good Spring Church Road. Take this little-used in-and-out road to a dead end where Good Spring Church and its attendant cemetery lie, along with a trailhead. This area sheds light on pre-park days, when what are now woods around you were simple farms from a simpler time. These families were bought out and relocated outside the current park boundaries. Return to Maple Springs Loop Road and turn left, rejoining Green River Ferry Road as it passes the park border at Stockholm and soon reaches Little Jordan Road/Ugly Creek Road at 9 miles.

Turn right here onto the gravel track that skirts the park boundary. Take your time on this road, likely the least used road in the entire park, passing over inappropriately named Ugly Creek on a low-water bridge. Pass the White Oak Trailhead on your right at 13 miles. This path leads down to the Green River on the old Dennison Ferry Road. Beyond the White Oak Trail, Little Jordan Road becomes Dennison Ferry Road; it's paved as it leaves the park and reaches Highway 1827 at 15 miles. Turn left here onto Highway 1827, passing through rural rolling farm- and pastureland with cattle and horses aplenty. At 20 miles the route intersects Highway 1352, which leads left back to the park visitor center across Green River Ferry. A country store is located here.

A mile from this intersection off Highway 1827, you'll reach Ollie Road; a sign indicates LINCOLN TRAILHEAD. Turn left here onto Ollie Road. Continue through south-central Kentucky backwoods and agricultural land on the park's edge. At 23 miles Ollie Ridge Road leaves right; you continue forward onto gravel Houchins Ferry Road, reentering the park completely. This ridge-running track passes the First Creek Trailhead, Temple Hill Trailhead, and pioneer cemeteries amid woodland to the actual Houchins Ferry at 29 miles.

Take this short boat trip, which operates from 10:15 A.M. to 6:00 P.M. daily, crossing back over to the south side of the Green River. A nice sheltered picnic area is located on the south side of the ferry, along with primitive Houchins Ferry campground. Beyond the ferry, the route passes through part of the small town of Brownsville, seat of Edmonson County. It has a few small mom-and-pop eateries and stores, and is nearly free of chain-type restaurants. If you want to see Brownsville, turn right instead of left at the junction with Highway 70, a mile from Houchins Ferry. This scenic drive, however, turns left onto Highway 70 and follows it to a second left turn, staying with Highway 70 and signs for Mammoth Cave National Park, which you'll soon reenter.

At 40 miles pass the Turnhole Bend Trailhead, which makes a nice short walk to a vista of the Green River and passes some sinks. Just beyond this trail, a right turn off Highway 70 onto Cedar Sink Road will soon lead to the Cedar Sink Trail, one of the park's best spring wildflower venues. At 41 miles the scenic drive reaches Mammoth Cave Parkway. A left turn on the parkway will lead back to the visitor center. Turn right to continue the scenic drive, reaching Sloans Crossing Pond on your right, which makes an excellent leg-stretching short walk.

Come to Park City Road at 43 miles, which leads right, to Interstate 65. Keep forward on Highways 255/70, reaching a T-intersection and the boundary limits of Cave City at 45 miles. Turn left here onto Highway 255, passing Mammoth Cave Canoe and Kayak, which offers float trips on the Green River. Reenter the park before reaching Sand Cave, the locale where famed cave explorer Floyd Collins was trapped for more than two weeks in 1925—a saga that brought the region national fame and led to the creation of Mammoth Cave National Park. A short all-access interpretive trail here leads to the mouth of Sand Cave, where a nation waited and thousands gathered to hear the fate of one of the greatest cavers ever to have lived.

Look for the right turn onto Park Ridge Road just beyond Sand Cave. The paved but wooded road makes for a pleasant cruise. Stay left as R Hunter Road veers right. Park Ridge Road ends at 51 miles. Turn right onto paved Flint Ridge Road, which makes for a quiet rural mile-long drive on the park boundary, past farmlands to reach the south-of-Green-River part of Dennison Ferry Road. Turn left onto gravel Dennison Ferry Road to reach a quiet picnic area beside the river, where paddlers launch canoes and kayaks for a pleasant float down the green Green. Only the name remains from the days when a ferry shuttled travelers across the river at this point.

Backtrack from Dennison Ferry Road, this time turning right onto Flint Ridge Road and staying with it as it heads west toward the visitor center. You'll pass Mammoth Cave Baptist Church, where Floyd Collins worshiped and is now buried. At 61 miles, return to the visitor center, completing your scenic auto loop.

Exploring Aboveground: The Rivers

The Green River and its major area feeder stream, the Nolin River, are the centerpieces of watery recreation at Mammoth Cave National Park. Along these waterways you can fish, paddle, and motorboat within the confines of the national park. Paddlers can ply the easy waters of both rivers, and fishing for warm-water species is undertaken by locals and visitors alike. Swimming in the park is generally discouraged: River access is difficult from the banks, and ferry traffic intrudes on potential swimming areas. Most park swimming is undertaken by people pulling their boats up to streamside gravel bars, then wading in.

The scenery of the Green and Nolin Rivers is fine—the Green River through Mammoth Cave National Park is a designated Kentucky Wild River. The riverine perspective helps put together the pieces of the puzzle of how Mammoth Cave came to be. Not only are these waters a recreation destination for visitors, but water is what created the cave, and thus the park. As waters seeped through the sandstone cap rock of cave country, they slowly dissolved the layer of limestone underneath, creating Mammoth Cave. The Green River then continued to cut an ever-deeper valley through time, creating layer after layer of cave. Today this process continues over nature's time and pace.

The Green River cuts an impressive valley through the hills of Kentucky's cave country.

Canoeing and Kayaking

The Green River is one of Kentucky's largest, longest, and most navigable rivers. Its headwaters are in southwestern Lincoln County near the town of Liberty, and it flows west into Green River Lake. From there the river is freed once again and flows westerly through Mammoth Cave National Park before ending its run at the Ohio River across from Evansville, Indiana.

The Green is one of the most biologically rich rivers in the country, and reportedly the fourth most biologically diverse in the world. It is a place where habitats of the North meet habitats of the South. Approximately 150 species of fish call the Green River home. The banks, alternating rock and mud, rise steeply from the water and meld into junglesque shores of thick forests that often obscure white limestone bluffs reaching upward for the Kentucky sky. The Green River has been and still is integral in the creation of Mammoth Cave, continually carving its valley. Waters flowing through sinkholes in the Mammoth Plateau above cut themselves deeper, creating new passages and leaving old dry ones as water continues to seek its level, aided by gravity and time. Today the Green flows through the heart of the national park, offering visitors an opportunity to float a canoe or kayak along this waterway, gaining new vantage points for enjoying the park—from the river looking outward to green cathedrals, to cave country catacombs where tours are undertaken and passages remain yet undiscovered, or below through the green waters at still logs fallen from the shore around which fish gather looking for their next meal. The portion of the Green River flowing through the national park is a state-designated Kentucky Wild River.

However, it is not only the Green River but also one of its tributaries, the Nolin River, that can be paddled within the confines of Mammoth Cave National Park. The Green River offers 20 miles of Class I paddling pleasure between park access points. It is rarely too low to paddle through the park, but excessive high water, also infrequent, can make it potentially dangerous. The Nolin River has 7 miles of watery meanderings to ply your boat. It also has Class I waters that flow through forested ridges reminiscent of Kentucky's great woodlands before the time of the pioneers. This lowermost part of the Nolin emerges from the Nolin River Lake Dam and runs its final miles to meet the Green at the western edge of the park.

Mussel Beaches

More than fifty species of mussels make their home in the Green River, including some of the rarest on earth. A trip along the river will reveal mussel shells embedded in the shallows as you float over them, and more shells on exposed gravel bars, creating a montage of white amid the tan pebbles left by previous year's high waters. By the way, mussels can live up to a hundred years. Please do not disturb them.

A mussel shell on the Green River.

Autumn is a great time to paddle the Green River.

The westernmost portion of the Green as well as much of the Nolin River in the park are slowed and affected by Lock 6, a dam and lock that was finished in 1906. Lock 6 is located on the western border of the park. The dam is still intact, but leaks, while the lock is entirely abandoned and no longer used or maintained. The Army Corps of Engineers recommends dismantling the lock, but no one yet knows when this will occur.

A note to park paddlers: Green River Ferry and Houchins Ferry are operating ferries that shuttle vehicles across the river. While launching or taking your boat out of the water, stay out of the way of the ferries. Launch and land your craft on the downstream side of the ferry, for safety's sake. Canoe camping is allowed throughout the park, but a free backcountry camping permit must be obtained from the rangers at the visitor center. Deadfalls are the only navigational river hazards.

Green River: Dennison Ferry to Green River Ferry

PADDLING DISTANCE: 7.5 miles

PADDLING TIME: 3–4 hours

RIVER LEVEL: 200 cubic feet per second, less than 10 feet

FEET PER MILE GRADIENT: 1

PADDLE SHUTTLE: To reach the take-out from the visitor center, take Mammoth Cave Parkway 0.6 mile. Turn right onto Green River Ferry Road and follow it for 1.3 miles to Green River Ferry. To reach the put-in at Dennison Ferry, return to the visitor center and turn right, easterly, onto Flint Ridge Road; follow this for 4.6 miles. Turn left onto gravel, dead-end Dennison Ferry Road and follow it for 1.5 miles to the put-in at the end.

The Green River enters the park at its confluence with Cub Run, then flows through the national park for 4 miles before reaching Dennison Ferry. The nearest upstream access is at Munfordville, at a city park on the north side of the U.S. Highway 31W bridge. It's 21 miles from Munfordville to Dennison Ferry. Practically speaking, the park portion of the river begins at Dennison Ferry, where the park has installed a canoe and kayak launch. The Green flows through the heart of cave country, and at least two caves can be scouted at water's edge. A small cave located 0.25 mile downstream of Dennison Ferry on the left bank can actually be paddled into for approximately 40 feet. This cave is known as Pike Spring. Three Sisters Island is located not far downstream. Floating Mill Island is at 6 miles.

The river scenery offers forested banks, while the river itself offers short shoals bordered by gravel bars between slower sections. Limestone bluffs border the river but are often obscured by the thickly wooded sides of the river valley. This section of the Green River is the most popular run in the park and is the primary day trip undertaken by visitors. Wildlife is abundant, with great variety visible to the careful observer. Channeled by the steep surrounding hills, the river averages 70 to 100 feet wide until it reaches Green River Ferry. Also, look for cave springs emanating from the banks, especially toward the end of the run. On the left bank, the River Styx and Echo River flow forth from the depths of Mammoth Cave.

Canoers paddle into Pike Spring Cave along the Green River.

Green River: Green River Ferry to Houchins Ferry

PADDLING DISTANCE: 12.2 miles

PADDLING TIME: 5–7 hours

RIVER LEVEL: 180 cubic feet per second, less than 10 feet

FEET PER MILE GRADIENT: 0.6

CAUTION: *To avoid the dangerous lock and dam, end your trip at Houchins Ferry or prepare to portage around the dam. Do not go over the dam.*

PADDLE SHUTTLE: To reach the Houchins Ferry take-out from the visitor center, take Mammoth Cave Parkway south for 2.9 miles to a split in the road. Veer right onto Highway 70, Brownsville Road. Follow this road for 9.7 miles to an intersection. Turn right here and stay with Highway 70 for 0.3 mile. Turn right on Houchins Ferry Road and follow it for 1.8 miles north to the Green River. To reach the put-in, backtrack almost all the way to the visitor center, then turn left onto Green River Ferry Road and follow it to the river.

From Green River Ferry, the river winds westward with a very slack current during normal flow. About a mile beyond the ferry and 200 feet off the river to your left is a small cave with a beautiful, clear pool of icy water. This is known as Bat Cave, or Blowing Cave. The river passes around large named islands such as Sand Cave Island and Boardcut Island. Sand Cave Island comes 3.7 miles beyond Green River Ferry. Watch for Sand Cave, visible from river left while passing Sand Cave Island. It's but a short walk from the river's edge to Sand Cave. Turnhole Bend, with its large pool to the left of the main river, is another point of interest at 4.5 miles. Look for the tall bluff and Turnhole Spring just beyond the pool of Turnhole Bend. Stice Island is at 6.5 miles. Buffalo Creek will flow in at 9 miles on your right. In another 3 miles you'll reach Houchins Ferry, the recommended take-out point for this particular trip.

Near Houchins Ferry, the Green broadens to 130 feet as it encounters the backwater pool of Brownsville Lock and Dam 6. The abandoned lock and dam lie outside the park, 3 miles below Houchins Ferry. *Caution:* This spot can be hazardous and must be portaged. Do not go over the dam! A take-out is located in Brownsville on the south side of the Highway 70 bridge. To access the boat ramp on Highway 70, turn right at the courthouse in Brownsville on Main Cross Street, then turn left onto Washington Street. Follow Washington Street under the Highway 70 bridge to end at Brownsville boat ramp.

Turn, Turn, Turn

Turnhole Bend got its name from the days when steamboats traveled up the Green River, taking tourists to Mammoth Cave. The upper river near the cave was so narrow that the steamboats could not turn around on the return journey. Therefore, upon leaving Mammoth Cave, they had to back down the river for several miles until reaching the wide "hole" in the river to turn around—hence *Turnhole Bend*.

The view from Turnhole Bend Overlook.

Green River Levels

To find the paddling status of the Green, check the gauge at Green River Ferry, located on the south side of the river. It should read less than 6 feet for safe paddling. This gauge is offset 4 feet from the USGS gauge at the same location, Green River at Mammoth Cave. So if the physical gauge at Green River Ferry is reading 2.7, then the USGS gauge on the Internet will read 6.7. This offset is done to prevent negative river readings. Another helpful gauge is the USGS "Green River at Munfordville." On the Internet, type in http://waterdata.usgs.gov/nwis/rt, then click on Kentucky, then find Green River at Munfordville. The water level should be at least 180 cfs for the lower section and 200 for the upper section. The Green River at Mammoth Cave gauge can also be found via the above Internet address. Furthermore, the water release information for Green River Lake Dam, located upstream of the national park, can be obtained by calling (270) 465–8824.

Nolin River: Nolin River Lake Dam to Houchins Ferry on the Green River

PADDLING DISTANCE: 9.1 miles

PADDLING TIME: 5 hours

RIVER LEVEL: Less than 10 feet

FEET PER MILE GRADIENT: 1

PADDLE SHUTTLE: To reach the take-out from the park visitor center, take Mammoth Cave Parkway south for 2.9 miles to a split in the road. Veer right onto Highway 70, Brownsville Road, and follow it for 9.7 miles to an intersection. Turn right here, staying with Highway 70 for 0.3 mile. Turn right onto Houchins Ferry Road and follow it for 1.8 miles north to the Green River. To reach the put-in, backtrack on Houchins Ferry Road to Highways 259/70 and turn right, cross the Green River, then continue north on Highway 259 (Highway 70 leaves left on the way) to Highway 728. Turn right onto Highway 728 and follow it for 2 miles to reach the Tailwater Recreation Area boat ramp.

Dismal Rock is located just across the river from the Tailwater boat ramp, the run's beginning. The Nolin River flows from the bottom of Nolin River Lake Dam, passing fields and wooded hillsides. The lowermost banks near the dam reflect sporadic large releases from Nolin River Lake Dam. Vegetation here will show signs of occasional inundation.

Enter the national park after 1.3 miles and an easterly turn. The park border is signed. The river, 50 to 80 feet wide, winds its way south in the northwestern wooded valley of Mammoth Cave and has a lazy current. You will pass the bluffs of Bylew Creek on your left at 2.2 miles. Here the Nolin is especially scenic, with high, exposed overhanging bluffs and plentiful wildlife, particularly deer and ducks. Overhanging silver maples and sycamores shade the stream. Camping areas must be scouted but can be found on flats above the river and at the mouths of incoming creeks.

The river widens as it comes closer to the Green. Pass Second Creek at 4.9 miles and First Creek at 6 miles. The actual Nolin River paddle section is 7.3 miles to the confluence with the Green River. At this point nearly all paddlers

The Nolin River has many overhanging bluffs, which add to an already scenic paddle.

Nolin River Levels

The Nolin below the Nolin River Lake Dam is runnable year-round. However, check the Army Corps of Engineers Nolin River Lake Web site; go to "Lake Levels," then see the "6 A.M. outflow" for Nolin (under the Green River Basin) and get the cubic-feet-per-second release from the dam. The minimum should be 200.

take on the easy 1.8-mile paddle upstream on the Green to the take-out at Houchins Ferry. Alternatively, you can head downstream on the Green River and take out 3 miles below the confluence with the Green in Brownsville, just below the Highway 70 bridge; along the way, however, you will have to portage the hazardous Lock and Dam 6. The Brownsville boat ramp is located on the south side of the river.

A Mammoth Cave National Park backcountry camping permit is required for overnight stays. The level of difficulty is Class I. Deadfalls are the only navigational hazard.

Motorboating

Small johnboats are by far the most commonly used motorboat in Mammoth Cave. They are primarily used by casual anglers on the lower Green River in the west side of the park. Here the waters are slowed and kept deeper by Lock and Dam 6, located near Brownsville. Despite the leaky state of this abandoned lock, it still holds back enough water to slack the flow of the Green and Nolin on the western edge of the park. The upper Green has too many shallows and shoals to run a johnboat. Larger boats are virtually nonexistent here, and their use would be unwise—the waters aren't large enough. Snags and other obstacles pose additional impediments. There are no suitable waterskiing or tubing location in the park.

When launching your johnboat, you can use Houchins Ferry Road, which leads directly into the water. Alert the ferry operator before you try to back your boat in, and he will stay on the far side of the river with the ferry. Johnboats can be taken far up the Nolin River, too, because no shoals block the stream, and it's plenty deep. A boat could also be launched at Green River Ferry, but that area is much busier; also, johnboats can only go downstream from there, because waters become too shallow upstream at Cave Island. Just below Nolin River Lake Dam, Tailwaters Recreation Area has a boat launch that could be used by johnboats as well for tooling around the Nolin River.

Scenic Boat Rides

A unique and interesting way to see Mammoth Cave National Park is to ply the Green River on the *Miss Green River II*. This is a 63-foot twin-diesel-powered vessel that seats up to 122 passengers. The passenger area is roofed, but has big windows on all sides to allow passengers views of the Green. A small deck on the front allows unobstructed views. Boat tours last around an hour.

The *Miss Green River II* was designed to replicate an old steamboat like those that once brought passengers from as far as Evansville, Indiana, to Mammoth Cave. It leaves Green River Ferry and heads downstream. Enjoy the bottom-up approach as you travel beneath the cliffs and woods of the Green River Valley. The boat is operated by a captain; a tour guide gives a short narrative history of the Green and points out wildlife and other features along the river, such as Bat

The view from inside the Miss Green River II.

Miss Green River II Trip Schedule

April and May
12:30 P.M., 2:00 P.M., 3:30 P.M.
Sunset Cruise 5:30 P.M.

June and July
11:00 A.M., 12:20 P.M., 1:45 P.M.,
   3:10 P.M., 4:30 P.M.
Sunset Cruise 6:00 P.M.
Twilight Cruise 7:15 P.M.

August through Labor Day
11:00 A.M., 12:20 P.M., 1:45 P.M.,
   3:10 P.M., 4:30 P.M.
Sunset Cruise 6:00 P.M.

September through October 10
12:00 P.M., 2:15 P.M., 4:00 P.M.
Sunset Cruise 5:30 P.M.

October 11 through October 26
11:30 A.M., 1:30 P.M., 3:15 P.M.
Sunset Cruise 4:30 P.M.

Cave and Ganter Cave. The boat turns around near Sand Cave Island and returns to Green River Ferry.

The tour is especially rewarding for the very young and old and those who cannot physically get around too much; however, a set of steps must be walked to reach the boat from shore. I enjoyed the tour myself much more than I'd expected, in all honesty. It operates from April through October, but occasionally opens in late March. The tour is quite busy from Memorial Day through Labor Day, with another upsurge during the peak leaf-viewing season, which is a good time to cruise the river. For reservations call (270) 758–2243.

Fishing

The Green and Nolin Rivers are the watery venues for anglers who visit the park. Fishermen do not need a license within the confines of the park, but do need to follow Kentucky creel limits, which vary from year to year. For the latest creel limits, check on the Internet at http://fw.ky.gov/fishlimits.asp. The primary species fished along these rivers are smallmouth bass, largemouth bass, rock bass (redeye), bream, and catfish. Muskellunge and walleye are also present in the Green River but are difficult to catch. Sloans Crossing Pond has no fish, but First Creek Lake does offer still-water angling opportunities.

By far the best way to fish is from a canoe, kayak, or small johnboat. Bank fishing is difficult at best, and locations are hard to find due to steep banks on the river as well as very limited river accesses. The two river accesses with working ferry operations, Green River Ferry and Houchins Ferry, are not places to bank fish, as anglers end up being in the way of ferries and boats entering and leaving the river.

That said, anglers in boats have many opportunities to toss in a line on the Green and Nolin. Johnboats prefer launching at Houchins Ferry and fishing the lower Green and Nolin Rivers, where the water is deep, the current is slow, and obstructions are few, should they choose to put a motor on their boat. The upper Green is more free flowing with pools and shallow shoals flowing over and alongside gravel bars, making the area better for canoe or kayak fishing.

River fishing with lures can be exciting—when the conditions are good. For starters, the Green River has to be green (rather than muddy, as after a heavy

First Creek Lake offers fishing and camping opportunities.

rain), especially in early spring. The most popular lures to use are spinners and small plugs. For spinners, I recommend Panther Martins, gold or silver, in either ¼-ounce or ⅛-ounce size, with an orangish tail. Crawdads are a mainstay of many game fish in the rivers here, so a floater/diver Rebel-brand crawfish plug is a good choice, as it initially floats on the surface, sometimes attracting top-water hits, then wiggles its way down, attracting fish all the while. A floating gold-colored Rapala is decent for top water and good on the reel. A better top-water choice is a Heddon-brand surface plug, especially the kind resembling a frog. These Heddons have a little circular noisemaking blade on the back, which can bring the fish in.

Mornings and evenings are best for plugs, whereas the middle of the day will be better spent using spinners. These are generalizations, but they have worked for me on these rivers. Other fishermen will have their own secrets, and bait fishing is another matter altogether. Bait fishing is allowed on the rivers.

With lures, try still waters along riverside structure, such as rock banks, standing bankside trees, and fallen trees in the water. Some fish will be working in the deeper parts of riffles. Shallows and open mud banks are the least productive areas of the rivers.

Where to Lay Your Head

Mammoth Cave has been a tourist destination for nearly two centuries, and visitors have needed a place to stay. Facilities on offer run the gamut from undeveloped backcountry campsites all the way up to fine hotels. All these spots where explorers can lay their heads are detailed below.

Backcountry Campsites

The north side of the park, where backcountry trails course through the hills and hollows on the north side of the Green River, has twelve backcountry campsites for overnight backpackers and equestrians.

Bluffs

NEAREST TRAILHEAD ACCESS: Good Spring Church
ON WHICH TRAIL: Good Spring Loop Trail
NEAREST WATER: Within 50 yards
NEAREST CONNECTING TRAILS: Buffalo Trail, Collie Ridge Trail

This pretty campsite is set between a long bluff line above and a small stream below. The site, beside a large boulder, is mostly level, and has a metal fire ring,

The Bluffs campsite is set on a level bench with a flowing stream below and over-hanging bluffs above.

a tent pad, leveled wood benches, and a lantern post. There is no hitching post, as horses are not allowed on the access trail to the campsite or at the campsite. Water can be had from the creek below the campsite or a drip line from the bluff above the campsite. The spur trail to the campsite from Good Spring Loop Trail—which actually passes along and under the bluff line—is 0.2 mile long.

Collie Ridge

NEAREST TRAILHEAD ACCESS: First Creek
ON WHICH TRAIL: Collie Ridge Trail
NEAREST WATER: Within 50 yards

NEAREST CONNECTING TRAILS: Good Spring Loop Trail, McCoy Hollow Trail, Wet Prong–McCoy Hollow Connector Trail

The Collie Ridge campsite is located in a flat above lowermost Wet Prong Buffalo Creek. The access trail winds down from Collie Ridge to reach the flat. On the way down you will hear your water source, a spring that pours forth from the hillside down which you walked. The campsite has a tent pad, fire ring, and lantern post. The spring is a short walk from the camping area. You can also access lower Wet Prong for exploring from the campsite.

Ferguson

NEAREST TRAILHEAD ACCESS: First Creek
ON WHICH TRAIL: Wet Prong of Buffalo Loop Trail
NEAREST WATER: Within 50 yards
NEAREST CONNECTING TRAILS: Blair Spring Trail, Collie Ridge Trail

This campsite overlooks a tributary of Wet Prong Buffalo Creek. The access trail angles uphill from the Wet Prong of Buffalo Loop Trail, curves around a ridge, then dips to reach the hillside camp after 0.2 mile. Amenities include a tent pad, metal fire ring, lantern post, and horse-hitching rack uphill from the camp. The level tent pad is the only flat spot at the camp. The fire ring is set on slightly sloping ground. Water can be accessed by walking down a draw to reach a creek in the small bottom below.

First Creek 1

NEAREST TRAILHEAD ACCESS: Temple Hill
ON WHICH TRAIL: First Creek Trail
NEAREST WATER: Within 50 yards
NEAREST CONNECTING TRAIL: McCoy Hollow Trail

Situated by First Creek Lake and the outflow of First Creek Lake, this level, popular campsite is shaded by maples. The usual amenities are here: tent pad, lantern post, log benches, metal fire ring, and horse-hitching post. The area between the lake and the campsite is open to the sun. The lake is below the campsite on a bluff and is a little hard to access directly from the camp. Water can be had from the lake; even better, however, is a slow dripping spring (which may go dry) located at the intersection of the spur trail to the First Creek 2 campsite and the First Creek Trail, which is around the south side of the lake. First Creek 1 campsite is within sight of the First Creek Trail.

First Creek 2

NEAREST TRAILHEAD ACCESS: Temple Hill
ON WHICH TRAIL: First Creek Trail
NEAREST WATER: Within 50 yards
NEAREST CONNECTING TRAIL: McCoy Hollow Trail

This large, level campsite is set on the shores of First Creek Lake and shaded by maple and tulip trees. A metal fire ring, tent pad, lantern post, and log benches complement the level setting, where the lake can be seen and is within 30 yards of the campsite. A short trail leads down to the lake. A horse-hitching post is on the uphill side of the camp. Water can be had from the lake; even better, however, is a slow dripping spring (which may go dry) located at the intersection of the spur trail to the campsite and the First Creek Loop Trail. The spur trail to the campsite from First Creek Loop Trail is 0.1 mile.

Homestead

NEAREST TRAILHEAD ACCESS: Good Spring Church
ON WHICH TRAIL: Good Spring Loop Trail
NEAREST WATER: Within 150 yards
NEAREST CONNECTING TRAIL: Turnhole Bend Trail

This is the closest and easiest backcountry campsite to access from an auto trailhead. The spur trail to reach it is only 0.6 miles from the Good Spring Church Trailhead. The campsite is on a level area that is somewhat open and bordered by shade trees. The campsite has a metal fire ring, lantern post, log benches, tent pad, and horse-hitching rack. The land drops off to the north toward Dry Prong. If you look off this north edge, you'll see a rock that juts out, which you can stand on. Below this rock, a spring is visible below. The land is too steep just below the rock, so you must work your way down along more foot-friendly slope. Water can also be had from small branches on the way in from the Good Spring Trailhead, or—since it's only 0.6 mile—you could carry your water in. The access trail is 0.2 mile from the Good Spring Loop Trail.

McCoy Hollow

NEAREST TRAILHEAD ACCESS: Temple Hill

ON WHICH TRAIL: McCoy Hollow Trail

NEAREST WATER: 0.8 mile

NEAREST CONNECTING TRAIL: McCoy Hollow–Wet Prong Connector Trail

This pretty campsite is high in the hills above the Green River, perched on the edge of a long drop-off leading down to the waterside. Cedars, hickories, and oaks shade the ridge-running camp, which is equipped with a metal fire ring, lantern post, tent pad, log benches, and horse-hitching rack. Campers need to bring their water to the campsite. The Green River is very far and steep below, and the river water is not recommended unless there are no alternatives. However, streams cross the McCoy Hollow Trail 1.3 miles to the south of the trail junction, toward Temple Hill, and 0.8 mile to the north, toward Wet Prong. No matter which direction you come from, bring a water carrier and access your water from one of these streams before reaching the dry camp.

Raymer Hollow

NEAREST TRAILHEAD ACCESS: Lincoln

ON WHICH TRAIL: Raymer Hollow Trail

NEAREST WATER: Within 50 yards

NEAREST CONNECTING TRAILS: Blair Spring Trail, Collie Ridge Trail

This campsite is situated on a hillside overlooking upper Dry Prong. The site is somewhat sloped, but it has a leveled tent pad along with a metal fire ring, leveled long seats, lantern post, and horse-hitching post. Water is located down below the campsite from Dry Prong. The creekside along Dry Prong is bordered with interesting rock bluffs and overhangs that are worth checking out. It is located 4.3 miles from Maple Springs Loop Road via the Raymer Hollow Trail, or 3.3 miles from the Lincoln Trailhead via Collie Ridge Trail and the west end of the Raymer Hollow Trail. The spur trail to the campsite from Raymer Hollow Trail is 0.3 mile.

Sal Hollow

NEAREST TRAILHEAD ACCESS: Maple Springs
ON WHICH TRAIL: Sal Hollow Trail
NEAREST WATER: 0.8 mile
NEAREST CONNECTING TRAILS: Buffalo Trail, Good Springs Loop Trail

This campsite is set amid tall trees on a hillside above Sal Hollow. There is an enormous beech tree adjacent to the campsite, which is shaded by oaks, maples, and other beech trees. It's slightly sloped but does have a level tent pad, metal fire ring, lantern post, and level wooden benches. It does not have a horse-hitching post—horses are not allowed on the Sal Hollow Trail. Water is a problem here, but can be accessed at the creek that flows through Sal Hollow 0.8 mile distant via Sal Hollow Trail. The creek does run dry below the Sal Hollow Trail crossing and may go entirely dry during periods of drought; then you must continue down Sal Hollow to the Green River for water.

Second Creek

NEAREST TRAILHEAD ACCESS: First Creek
ON WHICH TRAIL: First Creek Trail
NEAREST WATER: 0.5 mile
NEAREST CONNECTING TRAIL: Wet Prong of Buffalo Loop Trail

This pretty campsite is situated on spur ridge overlooking the confluence of Second Creek and the Nolin River. The campsite is level. The land drops off toward the Nolin River. It has a tent pad, metal fire ring, leveled log benches, lantern post, and horse-hitching posts. Large beech trees shade the camp. Water can be had by backtracking on the access trail to reach First Creek Trail and descending to Second Creek, which becomes visible below after keeping downhill. It is 0.1 mile from the First Creek Trail via the spur trail to the campsite.

Three Springs

NEAREST TRAILHEAD ACCESS: Temple Hill
ON WHICH TRAIL: McCoy Hollow Trail
NEAREST WATER: Within 50 yards
NEAREST CONNECTING TRAIL: First Creek Trail

This campsite is set in a hollow close to the Green River. The level site is in a heavily wooded flat beside a small creek that flows into the Green River just downstream. Water can be accessed from the creek, and campers can walk down to the Green River to fish or swim, though the banks are steep and muddy. This desirable overnighting locale is located 0.8 mile from Houchins Ferry Road via the McCoy Hollow Trail. The spur trail to the campsite from McCoy Hollow Trail is 0.1 mile. The campsite has a metal fire ring, tent pad, lantern post, log benches, and horse-hitching rack.

The author and his family camping on a gravel bar along the Green River.

Turnhole Bend

NEAREST TRAILHEAD ACCESS: Maple Springs
ON WHICH TRAIL: Turnhole Bend Trail
NEAREST WATER: 0.5 mile
NEAREST CONNECTING TRAILS: Sal Hollow Trail, Buffalo Trail, Good Spring Loop Trail

This pretty campsite sits atop a knob above a bend in the Green River. It's located at the south end of the Turnhole Bend Trail. The camp is very level and is well shaded by hickory and oak trees. The land drops away from the camp on three sides. It is equipped with metal fire ring, lantern post, log benches, tent pad, and horse-hitching rack. The only real problem with this campsite is lack of water. The nearest source is 0.5 mile away—head down to the Green River via the old Turnhole Bend Trail, which can be followed from the junction of the official Turnhole Bend Trail and the spur trail to this campsite. The spur trail to the campsite from Turnhole Bend Trail is 0.1 mile.

White Oak

NEAREST TRAILHEAD ACCESS: Little Jordan Road/Ugly Creek Road
ON WHICH TRAIL: White Oak Trail
NEAREST WATER: 40 yards
NEAREST CONNECTING TRAILS: None

White Oak is a lone campsite on a trail that has no connections. Still, it's one of the most attractive campsites in the park. It is set on a level area about 75 feet above the Green River, across from the Dennison Ferry Picnic Area and boat-launch site. It is not accessible by foot from Dennison Ferry but could be accessed by boat. Foot access is via the White Oak Trail. Tall maples and sycamores shade the camping area. Don't miss the 300-plus-year-old sycamore just downhill from the site. The camp has a tent pad, fire ring, lantern post, sitting logs, and horse-hitching rack. Steep mud banks make accessing the Green River potentially troublesome, but the river is your water source for this campsite.

Campgrounds

Mammoth Cave National Park has three campgrounds within its bounds. Each has its own attributes. Headquarters Campground is the largest. Conveniently located in the heart of the park near the visitor center and other developed facilities, it's within walking distance of cave tours. Houchins Ferry Campground is located on the western edge of the park on the banks of the Green River. It's more primitive but is open year-round. Maple Spring is a group campground north of the Green River and is great for equestrians, scouts, and church groups.

Below is a comprehensive review of each campground, including when it's open, the number of campsites, what each site has, site assignment, facilities, and fees. A narrative follows, describing the campground setting and area activities, along with access directions.

Headquarters Campground

OPEN: March through November

INDIVIDUAL SITES: 111

EACH SITE HAS: Picnic table, fire ring, lantern post; some also have tent pad and mini table

SITE ASSIGNMENT: First come, first served, and by reservation

REGISTRATION: At campground entrance station

FACILITIES: Flush toilets, water spigots, camp store, laundry, and token-operated hot showers nearby

FEE: $16 per night

If you're going to come and camp at Mammoth Cave for a few days, why not do it at the campground that sits in the heart of the park and directly over parts of the cave? This facility is called Headquarters for a reason. It's strategically located near the visitor center, where most of the cave tours take place, and is the jumping-off point for almost everything else.

The campground is large, but is spread over a wide area that's more level than not. Pass the campground entrance station. The first loop on your left has campsites 1 through 10. These are of special note to tent campers—they're reserved for tent campers only. The sites have been reworked and gravel tent pads added. The next loop has campsites 11 through 53. Typical of the camping area, these sites are well shaded and roomy. Some are pull-through, which big rigs like. Be aware that there are no electrical hookups in the campground.

The author spent a lot of days at Headquarters Campground, while writing this guidebook.

The next area has campsites 54 through 90. This large loop starts out level then offers some vertical variation. The campsites in the rear of the loop, such as 76, 78, and 80, are the most desirable. The final loop, with sites 92 through 111, is the hilliest and is the most isolated area of the campground.

Heated and air-conditioned restrooms are conveniently spread through the campground. Showers are offered from the token-operated shower area near the park convenience store, which is just a walk away. Tokens are obtained from the store or the lodge front desk. A post office and laundry area are also located near the park store.

The campground entrance station is staffed by Park Service employees who are there to help. Overall, the campground has that old-time atmosphere of vacationers out to have a good time in a pretty setting, as it should be in national parks. The campground will fill up on summer weekends; reservations are recommended. Call (800) 365–2267, or visit www.reservations.nps.gov on the Internet.

If you stay at Headquarters Campground, you can put your car keys away and enjoy numerous nearby pursuits. The visitor center is a short walk away. Informative rangers can help you with just about any question you have regarding the park. Head over there to determine the length and difficulty of the cave tours in which you wish to endeavor.

A series of nature trails winds through the bluffs and bottomlands between the campground and the nearby Green River. The Green River Bluffs Trail offers views. Or see the cave entrance of Dixon Cave along the Dixon Cave Trail. See the outflow of the Echo River Springs down by the Green River. Mammoth Dome Sink is a large depression where water disappears to enter Mammoth Cave. These are all interesting features that demonstrate the relationship between aboveground rock and water, and the rock and water you see on cave tours. Springtime visitors will enjoy the bonus of a surprising wildflower display that rivals the Great Smoky Mountains National Park.

Houchins Ferry Campground

OPEN: Year-round

INDIVIDUAL SITES: 12

EACH SITE HAS: Picnic table, fire grate, lantern post with additional mini table on it

SITE ASSIGNMENT: First come, first served, no reservations

REGISTRATION: Self-registration on site

FACILITIES: Water spigot, vault toilets

FEE: $12 per night

ACCESS: To find Houchins Ferry Campground from the visitor center, take Mammoth Cave Parkway south for 2.9 miles to a split in the road. Veer right onto Highway 70, Brownsville Road, and continue 9.7 miles to an intersection. Turn right here, staying with Highway 70 for 0.3

Mammoth Cave's Camp Store

Mammoth Cave National Park features a camp store conveniently located between the Headquarters Campground and the hotel/visitor center. Marked SERVICE CENTER, the store offers ice, firewood, gasoline, newspapers, bread, camping supplies, ice cream, toiletries, and limited food as well as a post office. You can also purchase souvenirs, clothing, and knickknacks.

mile. Turn right onto Houchins Ferry Road and follow it for 1.8 miles north to the campground, which is on the Green River.

Houchins Ferry Campground is the only campground at Mammoth Cave National Park open year-round. It's located away from the bulk of the park's action, and is thus less visited and less used. A ferry operates adjacent to the campground, which is stretched out along a flat about 30 feet above the Green River. Hardwoods shade the camping area, which is backed by a steep hill rising away from the Green. The understory is open and grassy. A gravel loop road leads past the water spigot and screened vault toilets to enter the camping area. The initial eight sites are directly riverside. Landscaping timbers delineate each campsite. Come to a small auto turnaround, where a couple more campsites are situated and have the most privacy. The final two campsites are away from the river and are well distanced from each other. Across from the campground, there is a brick picnic pavilion with two fireplaces, which could come in handy on rainy days. With only twelve sites, this small recreation area can only get so busy. The campground fills on summer weekends. Anglers and locals make return visits.

It's 15 miles to the cave area and visitor center. This can be a plus if you want to be near it all—but not *in* it all. However, Temple Hill Trailhead, 2 miles distant across the Green River from Houchins Ferry, offers backcountry hiking. These paths travel by rivers, steep bluffs, sinkholes, waterfalls, and old homesites. From here the underused and underappreciated McCoy Hollow Trail drops off Temple Hill and comes alongside the Green River, passing a big rockhouse and the Three Springs area. Wind in and out of little valleys to a decent view from the McCoy Hollow backcountry campsite. The First Creek Trail descends, passing large boulders, and then comes along a bluff line with amazing spring wildflowers before reaching First Creek Lake. Here the trail splits and loops across the lake. The Wet Prong of Buffalo Loop Trail is 7 miles distant and also offers good wildflowers in spring. You will be surprised at the ruggedness of the overall terrain.

The Green River affords fishing and boating opportunities. Canoe liveries are listed on the campground information board. A total of 26 miles of the Green River flow through the national park. The scenery here rivals that of the trail system. Anglers can vie for bass, crappie, and bluegill. You do not need a Kentucky fishing license within the park boundaries, but you must comply with Kentucky creel limits. The lower part of the river near Houchins Ferry is slowed by a dam in Brownsville. This dam can be hazardous; portage around it.

Maple Springs Group Campground

OPEN: March through November

GROUP SITES: 7

EACH SITE HAS: Picnic tables, large fire grate, lantern post

SITE ASSIGNMENT: By reservation; call (800) 967–2283

REGISTRATION: Self-registration on site

FACILITIES: Water spigot, vault toilets

FEE: $30 per night

ACCESS: From the visitor center, cars should take Mammoth Cave Parkway 0.6 mile. Turn right onto Green River Ferry Road and follow it 3.4 miles to Maple Springs Loop Road. Turn left, the campground is on the left. Note that RVs may not use the park ferries. See the map or consult the visitor center for directions.

This large campground enjoys a big, level site and offers a variety of conditions among its seven group campsites. These sites are stretched along a U-shaped loop located of Maple Springs Loop Road.

Enter the loop road and campsite 0 is on your left. All the sites are located on the outside of the loop. This site, with concrete picnic tables, is reserved for day use only and not available for overnight rental. Of the seven actual campsites, sites 1 through 4 are reserved for horses only, and technically these four sites are considered a separate campground. Each of the first four sites also has a horse-hitching area in the woods below, as well as a horse trailer parking area. Campsite 1 is a bit sloped. A water spigot is across from this camp, as are new-generation vault toilets. Campsite 2 is more heavily shaded. Campsite 3 is surrounded by cedar trees, but open in the middle. Another water spigot, with an adjacent horse-hitching post, is located near these sites. Campsite 4 is shaded by hardwoods and is a little less than level. Campsite 5 is well shaded, too, and is across from another set of restrooms. Campsite 6 is an excellent site located beneath tall pines. Campsite 7 is large and may be one of the most heavily used among the group sites here. A group fire ring and gathering area with benches is located in this vicinity.

Reservations are required. They can be made by dialing the above number or going online at www.reservations.nps.gov. Group size is limited to twenty-four people per site. The campground is used by equestrians, scout groups, church groups, and large families. Campsites are always available in spring. In summer all seven sites are occupied three out of four weekends. Fall is the busiest time at this campground, and expect nice weekends to be full.

Maple Springs Group Campground is located on the north side of the Green River, but just a ferry boat ride away from the main park goings-on near the visitor center. Different groups seek their own activities, but cave tours are popular with nonequestrians, and the adjacent backcountry trails are popular with riders.

Accommodations

Mammoth Cave National Park's first on-site hotel was established in 1837, and the tradition continues to this day. Four overnighting options are offered by Forever Resorts, which is an authorized concessionaire of the National Park Service: the Mammoth Cave Hotel, Sunset Terrace, Historic Cottages, and Woodland Cottages. Each can be reserved by calling (270) 758–2225. Use this same number for exact rates as well as opening and closing dates, or visit www.mammothcavehotel.com. By the way, call the hotel for exact directions; Internet directions on such sites as Yahoo! are wrong, because the hotel does not have a physical address.

Mammoth Cave Hotel

Mammoth Cave Hotel is located literally a minute away from the park visitor center and is less than 300 feet from the Historic Entrance to Mammoth Cave. The hotel has forty-two rooms on two floors. These are basic hotel rooms, with heat, air-conditioning, telephones, and a television. Each room has a small deck with chairs.

The hotel is open year-round and has in-house eateries. It's busiest during summer, when reservations are recommended; it's less busy during the other seasons. Call for off-season rates and other special offerings. An ATM is located in the lobby. The hotel also has meeting facilities for up to 125 people.

Kennels

Mammoth Cave Hotel offers kennels for those wanting to keep their pets in comfort while they tour the cave. The service is free for hotel guests but charges a fee to others. Pet owners can leave their dog for four- or eight-hour increments. Separate stalls are provided for each animal. Bring your own bowl for your pet. Water spigots are provided. This service is first come, first served, but spaces are nearly always available. For more information, call the hotel at (270) 758–2225.

Sunset Terrace

Sunset Terrace is a single-story set of twenty rooms, where guests park their cars in front of their room door. Located near the hotel, these are larger than your average hotel rooms; they're often used by families. Sunset Terrace is located near the Heritage Trail and is within close proximity of the visitor center. Up to two children can stay free with adults in these rooms, which are open year-round.

Historic Cottages

The Historic Cottages are located on attractive grounds in the heart of the park, and are within walking distance of the visitor center. These ten wooden buildings, set in a horseshoe beneath shade trees, are original park structures. They have been modernized with heat, air-conditioning, and television, but no telephone. The buildings, each with one room and a bathroom, are most often rented by couples who want to be close to the action, but still maintain a little distance from that action. Each cottage also has a small porch with chairs. They are open from mid-March through October.

The Historic Cottages are original park structures.

Woodland Cottages

The Woodland Cottages, the most economical choice, are located next to the Headquarters Picnic Area and across the parking lot from the visitor center. There are twenty small wooden buildings located close to one another. They range in size from one to four rooms, though most are one room. They are rustic, with no air-conditioning, but they do have electricity, running water, and bathroom. These are often rented by groups or outdoorsy types who want "no-frills" accommodations. The Woodland Cottages are open from late April through September.

Area Bed-and-Breakfasts

For those who want a more refined overnighting experience in the national park area, I've described some local bed-and-breakfasts below, along with important contact information.

Cave Spring Farm Bed and Breakfast

P.O. Box 365
Smiths Grove, KY 42171
(270) 563–5863
www.bbonline.com/ky/cavespring/

Only 7 miles from the national park, this 1857 farm home—listed on the National Register of Historic Places—is situated on seventeen acres. There are rooms in the house, or you can stay in an old one-room schoolhouse, the Little House in the woods, or an old log cabin. Breakfast is served on fine china.

Rose Manor

204 Duke Street
Cave City, KY 42127
(270) 773–4402
www.mammothcave.com/rose.htm

This B&B is located in Cave City. Five rooms include the Amethyst Room, which has its own private Jacuzzi. Choose what time you want your unlimited served breakfast. Your hosts want you to feel like the king and queen while you are with them.

Serenity Hill

3600 Mammoth Cave Road (Highway 70)
Brownsville, KY 42210
(270) 597–9647
www.serenityhillbedandbreakfast.com
serenityhill@serenityhillbedandbreakfast.com

Located on the southwest side of the park and convenient to Brownsville, this hilltop B&B offers four rooms, including the bridal suite. The country house has large porches with views and an open deck.

The Wayfarer

1240 Old Mammoth Cave Road
Cave City, KY 42127
(270) 773–3366
www.bbonline.com/ky/wayfarer/
thewayfarer@scrtc.com

The Wayfarer is located on the edge of Mammoth Cave National Park. It offers five rooms within an attractive wood structure. The same owners also offer Hanson Cottage, a separate small house adjacent to the Wayfarer. Breakfast is served in the southern tradition. Innkeepers Larry and Becky Bull will make you feel at home here in Cave Country.

More Services and Resources for Explorers

Park visitors have an array of services available in the heart of the park, including an assortment of picnic areas, eateries, a gas station, and outdoor outfitters. I've also included pocket descriptions of nearby towns.

Picnic Areas

The park has several designated picnic areas to enjoy. Recreation opportunities are available near most picnic areas, enabling you to work off those hamburgers and hot dogs. The following is a list of these picnic areas, along with suggested area activities.

Mammoth Cave National Park Contact Information

Mammoth Cave National Park
Mammoth Cave, KY 42259
(270) 758-2180
www.nps.gov/maca
Tour reservations: (800) 365-2267 or www.reservations.nps.gov

---

Dennison Ferry

ACCESS: To find the Dennison Ferry Picnic Area from the visitor center, take Flint Ridge Road, a two-lane paved avenue, east for 4.6 miles to Dennison Ferry Road. Turn left and continue 1.5 miles to the picnic area at the end of this dead-end road.

This picnic area is situated in a little-visited east side of the park on the south side of the Green River. Site of a ferry operation from pre-park days, the area was once a campground but is now purely a picnic area. A grassy area on a flat above the Green River is shaded by hardwoods. Each of the picnic tables is accompanied by a sitting bench and grill. A porto john is located on site.

The primary recreation here centers on the Green River. A canoe and kayak launch leads down from the picnic area to the river. The launch has a boat slide to aid paddlers in getting their boats down to the river.

Headquarters

ACCESS: The Headquarters Picnic Area is located north of the visitor center parking area, near the Woodland Cottages.

Headquarters is by far the largest picnic area in the park. Adjacent to the visitor center parking lot, it also has the most facilities. Rolling terrain of grass with scattered oaks and hickories make for a naturally appealing setting. It's spread over many acres with picnic tables set in both sun and shade, but primarily in the shade. Many of the tables have accompanying grills.

There are two large reservable picnic shelters, compete with built-in fireplaces. These shelters require a fee if reserved but otherwise are free to use on a first-come, first-served basis. Furthermore, Headquarters Picnic Area also has an enclosed picnic shelter complete with windows for maximum protection from the elements; it's available only by reservation. The picnic area has water spigots and fully equipped restroom facilities.

Recreation possibilities are close and varied. The Green River Bluffs Trail leaves from the beginning of the loop portion of the picnic area and leads 0.6 mile to an overlook on the Green River; it connects to the Dixon Cave Trail, among other paths. The visitor center—within walking distance—is the jumping-off point for all cave tours, a must for park visitors. Interpretive ranger-led programs are ongoing at the visitor center.

Houchins Ferry

ACCESS: To locate the Houchins Ferry Picnic Area from the visitor center, take Mammoth Cave Parkway south for 2.9 miles to a split in the road. Veer right onto Highway 70, Brownsville Road. Follow Brownsville Road 9.7 miles to an intersection. Turn right, staying with Highway 70 for 0.3 mile to reach Houchins Ferry Road. Turn right and follow Houchins Ferry Road 1.8 miles north to the picnic area, on your right.

Houchins Ferry Picnic Area, on the banks of the Green River, is one of several facilities located at this western end of the park near Brownsville. The actual Houchins Ferry operates here, and Houchins Ferry Campground is just a few feet away across a road. The picnic area has covered and open facilities. A large pavilion with twin brick fireplaces at one end offers shade and rain protection

Houchins Ferry Picnic Area is located on the banks of the Green River.

for those wishing to relax here with a meal. Large stand-up grills are at the far end of the pavilion. There are also two open-air picnic tables, which are complemented by benches, lantern posts, and upright grills. Restroom facilities are available at the nearby campground. A water spigot is also here.

Fishing is the obvious recreational activity at Houchins Ferry. Otherwise visitors can take the ferry across the Green River to the Temple Hill and First Creek Trailheads and enjoy some of the trails. A good idea is the First Creek Trail, which descends from Temple Hill and the loops around First Creek Lake.

Maple Springs

ACCESS: To find the Maple Springs Picnic Area from the visitor center, head south on Mammoth Cave Parkway for 0.6 mile to Green River Ferry Road. Turn right onto Green River Ferry Road and follow it 1.3 miles to the Green River Ferry. After crossing the river, continue north on Green River Ferry Road for 2.1 miles to Maple Springs Loop Road. Turn left and drive 1 mile to the picnic area and trailhead on your right.

Maple Springs Picnic Area is located at the Maple Springs Trailhead, north of the Green River. Three picnic tables are sited in the grass-and-tree center of a parking loop suitable for hikers and equestrians. Restroom facilities are also available.

Since this picnic area is at a trailhead, hiking is a natural option. Take the Buffalo Trail west for an easy family walk. If you're feeling more energetic, continue on the Buffalo Trail, turn south at the Turnhole Bend Trail, and then take the Sal Hollow Trail back to the picnic area for a loop hike of 4.9 miles. While you are in the area, take the 0.5-mile drive to Good Spring Church, established before the park came to be. Other trails emanate from here.

Overlook

ACCESS: To find the Overlook Picnic Area from the visitor center, head south on Mammoth Cave Parkway for 2 miles to the picnic area on your left.

Overlook Picnic Area is located on Mammoth Cave Parkway, 2 miles from the visitor center. Visitors often stop here on their way into the park. There is but one picnic table here, and little to do in terms of active recreation. However, there is an overlook that offers great views from Mammoth Cave Ridge, site of the picnic area, into Doyel Valley, which was once cultivated and homesteaded. There are no restroom or cooking facilities.

Sloans Crossing

ACCESS: To find the Sloans Crossing Picnic Area from the visitor center, head south on Mammoth Cave Parkway for 2.9 miles to a road split. Stay left here, still on Mammoth Cave Parkway; the picnic area is on your immediate right.

Sloans Crossing Picnic Area is located on Mammoth Cave Parkway, not far from the intersection where the parkway veers right near its junction with Brownsville Road. Cedars and oaks shade the three wheelchair-accessible picnic tables located near an old homesite. There are no restroom or cooking facilities.

One of the park's most unusual interpretive trails starts at the picnic area, the Sloans Crossing Pond Walk. A 0.4-mile boardwalk circles this natural depression that was dammed and deepened in pre-park days. Benches and decks overlooking the pond allow those walking the boardwalk to gain closer looks at this pond.

Tailwaters

ACCESS: To reach the Tailwaters Picnic Area from the park visitor center, take Mammoth Cave Parkway south for 2.9 miles to a split in the road. Veer right onto Highway 70, Brownsville Road, and continue for 9.7 miles to an intersection. Turn right here and stay with Highway 70, which is joined by Highway 259. Pass through Brownsville and cross

Dining Facilities at Mammoth Cave National Park

The greater visitor center/hotel area has three restaurants for convenient dining at the heart of Mammoth Cave National Park. The Travertine is the main dining facility and seats 164. It serves breakfast, lunch, and dinner and is open year-round. Crystal Lake Coffee Shop is open for lunch year-round. Troglobites is a fast-food-type establishment open from June through Labor Day.

Concessionaire Contact Information

Mammoth Cave Hotel
Mammoth Cave National Park
P.O. Box 27
Mammoth Cave, KY 42259-0027
(270) 758-2225
www.mammothcavehotel.com

the Green River, continuing north on Highway 259 (Highway 70 leaves left on the way) to reach Highway 728. Turn right onto Highway 728 and follow it for 2 miles to reach the Tailwater Recreation Area boat ramp.

Tailwaters Recreation Area is located just outside Mammoth Cave National Park. Part of Nolin River Lake, it's run by the Army Corp of Engineers. It's included in this guidebook, however, because it's so close to the national park and is the jumping-off point for a national park adventure: canoeing the lowermost Nolin River. Set in the land just below Nolin River Lake Dam, it has a riverside picnic area shaded by sycamore trees, and a large covered picnic area. Restrooms are on site.

The primary recreation here centers on the Nolin River. A fishing platform is located by the dam outlet. A boat launch is located on the Nolin River. A horseshoe pit is located by the boat launch. The recreation area also has a playground for children.

Nearby Towns

The following towns are all within a stone's throw (so to speak) of the national park, and are all worth exploring either for the critical facilities and resources they offer, or simply for their own unique charms.

Bowling Green

The area's largest city, Bowling Green is located about 40 miles southwest of Mammoth Cave National Park. This city is the home of Western Kentucky University. It has a mall, two hospitals, big-box stores, hotels, and restaurants of every sizes and description. There are golf courses, too, but the city's biggest attraction is the National Corvette Museum. Chevrolet's Corvette Plant is located in the Bowling Green area. Warren County, where Bowling Green is located, is a "wet" county. For more information, visit www.bgky.org.

Brownsville

Brownsville is the seat of Edmonson County, where most of the park is located. It is a small, quiet town on the bluffs of the Green River, at the western edge of the park. Along with a small grocery store, small nonchain restaurants, and a few chain fast-food offerings, it features a library, banks, ATMs, and a relaxed atmosphere. Nolin River Lake is located northeast of town and is a recreation destination in its own right. For more information, visit www.cavesandlakes.com.

Cave City

Cave City is located just outside the park, on its southeastern flank, near Exit 53 on Interstate 65. Hotels and eateries are located just off the interstate, offering varied lodging and dining to suit most budgets. A little east of I–65, however, stands downtown, on a rise with its antiques stores and more. Cave City also has a convention center and seasonal farmers' market. For more information, visit www.cavecity.com.

Glasgow

Glasgow is approximately 20 miles south of Mammoth Cave and is the seat of Barren County. It has a hospital, library, full-size grocery and big-box stores, and restaurant offerings from fast food to sit-down establishments. Multiplex movie theaters are here as well. Downtown Glasgow, with its old-time businesses, is on the upswing—it's worth a visit. Nearby, Barren River Lake with a state park on its shores complements Mammoth Cave National Park. For more information, visit wwwglasgow-ky.com.

Park City

This sleepy town is located just east of Exit 48 on Interstate 65. It is a small community where many of Mammoth Cave National Park's employees live. It has a convenience store/gas station adjacent to the interstate, a hardware store, post office, and library.

Outfitters

Mammoth Cave National Park has four commercial outfitters licensed to operate within its bounds:

Big Buffalo Crossing Canoe and Kayak

P.O. Box 985
Munfordville, KY 42765
(270) 774–7883 or (866) 233–2690
www.bigbuffalocrossing.com

This outfit is situated in Munfordville, upstream of Mammoth Cave National Park on the Green River. It offers canoe and kayak trips on the upper Green, the Nolin, and the Green through the national park.

Double J Stables

542 Lincoln School Road
Mammoth Cave, KY
(270) 286–8167
www.doublejstables.com

Double J—located on the north border of the park, near the Lincoln Trailhead—offers guided rides from thirty minutes to eight hours long, as well as stables and camping for equestrians. A park trail connects the stables to the Collie Ridge Trail.

Green River Canoeing

1145 Main Street
Brownsville, KY 42210
(270) 749–2041
www.mammothcavecanoe.com

This group operates on the Green River between Munfordville and Houchins Ferry, including the sections through Mammoth Cave National Park. It also runs trips on the Nolin from below Nolin River Lake to the Green. Trips last from two hours to two days.

Mammoth Cave Canoe and Kayak

1240 Old Mammoth Cave Road
Cave City, KY 42127
(270) 773–3366 or (877) 592–2663
www.mammothcavecanoe-k.com

Located on the park border near Sand Cave, the staff at this friendly outfit offer canoe and kayak rentals, along with shuttles for the Green River within and beyond Mammoth Cave National Park boundaries. Their primary day trip is from Dennison Ferry to Green River Ferry. They will shuttle private canoes almost anywhere along the Green.

Volunteering

Mammoth Cave National Park needs your help! Volunteering is a rewarding way to give back to the places that you love. Not only are individuals encouraged to get involved, but so are groups. Contact the park at (270) 758–2180 and ask for the VIP coordinator.

Index

About the Author

Johnny Molloy is an outdoor writer based in Johnson City, Tennessee. A native Tennessean, he was born in Memphis and moved to Knoxville in 1980 to attend the University of Tennessee. It was in Knoxville that he developed a love of the natural world that has since become the primary focus of his life.

It all started on a backpacking foray into the Great Smoky Mountains National Park. That first trip, though a disaster, unleashed an innate love of the outdoors that has led to his spending more than a hundred nights per year in the wild, over the past twenty-five years, backpacking and canoe camping throughout our country.

After graduating from the University of Tennessee with a degree in economics, he spent an ever-increasing time in natural places, becoming more skilled in a variety of environments. Friends enjoyed his adventure stories; one even suggested he write a book. He pursued his friend's idea and soon he had parlayed his love of the outdoors into an occupation.

The results of his efforts are more than twenty-seven books, including hiking guidebooks, camping guidebooks, paddling guidebooks, comprehensive guidebooks about specific areas, and true outdoor adventure tales. Molloy's work has also appeared in numerous magazines and Web sites. He continues to write and travel extensively to all four corners of the United States, pursuing a variety of outdoor activities. For the latest on Johnny, please visit www. johnnymolloy.com.

FALCON GUIDE® *LEADING THE WAY*

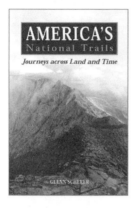

America's National Trails
Journeys across Land and Time
GLENN SCHERER

This book is a celebration of the 40,000-mile National Trails System. Through magnificent color photography and profiles of significant trails, this rare collection explores the amazing events and people that have helped shape America's historic and scenic trails. Discover the fascinating histories and delight in the beautiful scenery of the world's largest network of recreational trails.

Get Outside!
A Guide to Volunteer Opportunities and Working Vacations in America's Great Outdoors
AMERICAN HIKING SOCIETY

This one-of-a-kind directory describes thousands of volunteer opportunities across the country.

Learn how to:
▲ Become a wilderness patroller in wild high country
▲ Work as an interpretive guide at a historic lighthouse
▲ Conduct surveys of wildflowers
▲ Build a footbridge
▲ Develop an environmental curriculum

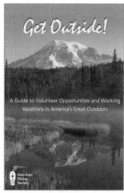

It's an invitation to exciting new experiences, a working contribution to our nation's great outdoors, and lasting memories for folks of all ages.

www.falcon.com

Falcon Trails on the Web

To learn more about Falcon or to get detailed information about our more than 10,000 published trails and routes, go to **www.falcontrails.com.** While there, purchase custom topo maps, view real-time weather, post and review trail reports, and much more.

THE INSIDER'S SOURCE

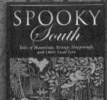

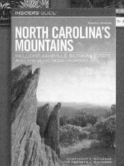

With more than 185 South-related titles, we have the area covered. Whether you're looking for the path less traveled, a favorite place to eat, family-friendly fun, a breathtaking hike, or enchanting local attractions, our pages are filled with ideas to get you from one state to the next.

For a complete listing of all our titles, please visit our Web site at www.GlobePequot.com. The Globe Pequot Press is the largest publisher of local travel books in the United States and is a leading source for outdoor recreation guides.

FOR BOOKS TO THE SOUTH

INSIDERS' GUIDE®

FALCON GUIDE®

Available wherever books are sold.
Orders can also be placed on the Web at www.GlobePequot.com, by phone from 8:00 A.M. to 5:00 P.M. at 1-800-243-0495, or by fax at 1-800-820-2329.

What's So Special about Unspoiled, Natural Places?

Beauty   Solitude   Wildness   Freedom   Quiet   Adventure
Serenity   Inspiration   Wonder   Excitement
Relaxation   Challenge

There's a lot to love about our treasured public lands, and the reasons are different for each of us. Whatever your reasons are, the national **Leave No Trace** education program will help you discover special outdoor places, enjoy them, and preserve them—today and for those who follow. By practicing and passing along these simple principles, you can help protect the special places you love from being loved to death.

The Principles of Leave No Trace

- Plan ahead and prepare
- Travel and camp on durable surfaces
- Dispose of waste properly
- Leave what you find
- Minimize campfire impacts
- Respect wildlife
- Be considerate of other visitors

Leave No Trace is a national nonprofit organization dedicated to teaching responsible outdoor recreation skills and ethics to everyone who enjoys spending time outdoors.

To learn more or to become a member, please visit us at www.LNT.org or call (800) 332-4100.

Leave No Trace, P.O. Box 997, Boulder, CO 80306

Other Books by Johnny Molloy

A Canoeing & Kayaking Guide to Florida

A Canoeing & Kayaking Guide to Kentucky (with Bob Sehlinger)

A Paddler's Guide to Everglades National Park

Beach & Coastal Camping in Florida

Beach & Coastal Camping in the Southeast

The Best in Tent Camping: The Carolinas

The Best in Tent Camping: Colorado

The Best in Tent Camping: Florida

The Best in Tent Camping: Georgia

The Best in Tent Camping: Kentucky

The Best in Tent Camping: Southern Appalachian & Smoky Mountains

The Best in Tent Camping: Tennessee

The Best in Tent Camping: West Virginia

The Best in Tent Camping: Wisconsin

Day & Overnight Hikes in Shenandoah National Park

Day & Overnight Hikes in the Great Smoky Mountains National Park

Day & Overnight Hikes in West Virginia's Monongahela National Forest

Day & Overnight Hikes: Kentucky's Sheltowee Trace

From the Swamp to the Keys: A Paddle Through Florida History

The Hiking Trails of Florida's National Forests, Parks, and Preserves
(with Sandra Friend)

Land Between the Lakes Outdoor Recreation Handbook

Long Trails of the Southeast

Mount Rogers Outdoor Recreation Handbook

50 Hikes in the North Georgia Mountains

50 Hikes in the North Georgia Mountains

50 Hikes in South Carolina

60 Hikes Within 60 Miles: Nashville

Trial by Trail: Backpacking in the Smoky Mountains

Visit the author's Web site:
www.johnnymolloy.com

A bellwort at Mammoth Cave National Park.

— *Notes* —

— *Notes* —